Conviviality in Bellville:
An Ethnography of Space, Place, Mobility and Being in Urban South Africa

Ingrid Brudvig

Langaa Research & Publishing CIG
Mankon, Bamenda

Publisher:
Langaa RPCIG
Langaa Research & Publishing Common Initiative Group
P.O. Box 902 Mankon
Bamenda
North West Region
Cameroon
Langaagrp@gmail.com
www.langaa-rpcig.net

Distributed in and outside N. America by African Books Collective
orders@africanbookscollective.com
www.africanbookcollective.com

ISBN: 9956-792-50-0

DISCLAIMER
All views expressed in this publication are those of the author and do not
necessarily reflect the views of Langaa RPCIG.

Table of Contents

iii

iv

Acknowledgements

The research that originally facilitated the data collection that led to this book benefitted from various sources of funding, including: the National Research Foundation (NRF) and the South Africa-Netherlands Research Programme on Alternatives in Development (SANPAD). Opinions expressed and conclusions arrived at are those of the author and are not necessarily to be attributed to the funding organizations.

I would like to thank Francis Nyamnjoh for the inspiration and support in conceptualizing this research and publication. His knowledge and guidance have led me to discover my true interest in topics related to migration, citizenship and belonging.

I also express tremendous gratitude to the staff of Scalabrini English School in Cape Town who have helped me become more active in the migrant community in Cape Town and were instrumental in helping me build relationships with the Somali Association of South Africa in Bellville. Deepest thanks and respect also extend to the Somali Association of South Africa, students at Scalabrini English School and Bellville Education Centre, Abdillahi Qorshe for his contribution to the photos included in this book, and countless other research participants whose conviviality I acknowledge with utmost appreciation.

I would like to thank my family across the world for their eternal support, interest in my research and patience towards my academic commitments. Thank you to mom especially for your insight and daily wise advice.

Figures & Vignettes

Introduction

This book takes place in a milieu characterized by human mobility, a global trend that is expressed through daily life in South Africa's urban public spaces. It sets out to examine the extent to which conviviality emerges amongst the diverse migrant and mobile population that frequents Bellville's central business district surrounding the train station, an area located approximately 25 kilometres from Cape Town. The Bellville train station and central business district, which are adjacent to the main Durban Road (see maps below), hosts a large and diverse population of both South Africans and foreigners - from countries including Somalia, Ethiopia, Ghana, Tanzania, Angola, Mozambique, Kenya, Jordan, Pakistan and Bangladesh amongst others - who have migrated to the area seeking work and income generating opportunities, such as informal trading, shop keeping, and other ad hoc livelihoods.

Many migrants have settled in Bellville to avoid negative attitudes and discrimination by South Africans in township areas in the aftermath of the 2008 xenophobic outbreaks. Recent unrest and violence towards non-nationals thus constitutes the backdrop for research at Bellville's central business district (CBD). While many South Africans who frequent Bellville come from the Western Cape Province – including Cape Town and surrounds – there is also a significant population of migrants from within South Africa who have moved to Cape Town from other provinces such as Gauteng and the Eastern Cape. Bellville is, therefore, a fitting site for this research, as it hosts similarly constituted migrant populations to other areas of Cape Town. It is in this context that I question what makes Bellville more accommodating to foreign migrants than other areas, such as township locations where many migrants face violent threats, daily insecurity and diminishing livelihood opportunities. What makes this particular zone in Bellville, and the South Africans that frequent there, different from their counterparts in the townships and other areas?

Embodied in the space of the Bellville CBD is its cumulative socio-economic history, influenced in recent years by international migrants, primarily from other African countries, who have migrated to Bellville over the past ten years. The social dynamics of Bellville are rooted in its diversity of nationalities, interwoven with a new collective narrative of migration now shared by the community. The order, routine and seeming stillness amidst chaos in Bellville's central business district symbolize, for me, the nature of a socialized place based on collectivity and conviviality, in which meaning and belonging are negotiated on the basis of a fine line of tolerance – catalysed or, perhaps imposed, by necessity. Bellville represents a symbiosis, an urban enclave where diverse networks of migrants have come together for business association and social cooperation, forming interdependent associations. The social fabric of this community-in-the-making is formed by an expanding and shared sense of mutual belonging. Furthermore, Somalis, who make up the majority of residents in Bellville's central business district, claim to feel safer there than elsewhere, such as in the townships of Cape Town. A sense of hope and aspiration pervades, and willingness, in face of need, to break old norms, create new opportunities and adapt to society.

1. 1 Mobilities and Social Life in Bellville

Mobility is definitive of social life in Bellville, rather than exceptional. Mobility is, in the words of Adey, "ubiquitous" (2010: 1). It is experienced all the time and in many different forms such as through transportation, daily routines in an around Bellville and by way of life histories that have become characterized by movement. While people move in and out of Bellville, services, information, capital and goods too become mobile (Adey, 2010: 3). This has created an infrastructure of mobility that is characteristic of "spaces of flows" (Adey, 2010: 11). Mobility is distinctive in Bellville both for those who come and go on a daily basis and for those who are – or have become – more or less "regulars" there. Bellville is a place of rapid movement and interchange of people, largely propelled by economic activities, daily transportation services and a myriad of other ways of getting by. The proximity of the field site to the train station (and inclusive of it) is vital to understanding social relations in Bellville as a mobile space. As Frank and Stevens note, "Railway stations are characteristic places for close and varied as well as anonymous and fleeting encounters" (2007: 78). Social relations in places of mobility become constituted through various entities, what Latour (cited in Urry, 2008: 13) calls "circulating entities" that bring about relationality within and between localities at varied distances. A community of migrants, local and global nomads so to speak, have culminated in a space that is symbolic of movement and transition informed by ideas of being, redefining Bellville in light of its multiple connections that cut across space, place and locality.

Migration to Bellville is often, but not exclusively, a survival response. The need to become mobile may be imperative when urban or rural residents endure insecurities that limit their access to basic needs through normal channels. As rural sustainable livelihoods become less viable, movement into cities becomes the norm. Further, without access to social welfare services, such as satisfactory medical and educational services, residents become uncommitted to locality in the long-term (Nyamnjoh and Brudvig, 2013). They may respond to emerging insecurities by moving more frequently and within short notice, whereby forging tactical alliances becomes due task (Murray and Myers 2006: 119). Despite family or other emotive commitments to locality, "home" becomes an encumbrance when it no longer serves critical needs (Nyamnjoh and Brudvig, 2013: 3). Conviviality emerges through the formation of tactual alliances, as they are often crafted out of mutual need – a reciprocity that holds great value in the context of urban anonymity.

Figure 1: Map of Bellville in Relation to Cape Town Metropolitan Area

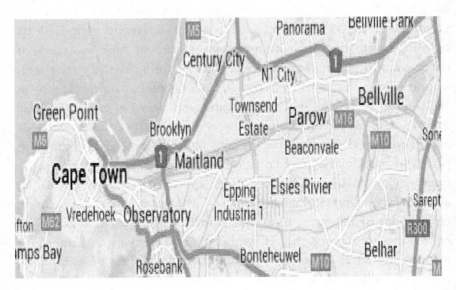

Figure 2: Map of Research Area

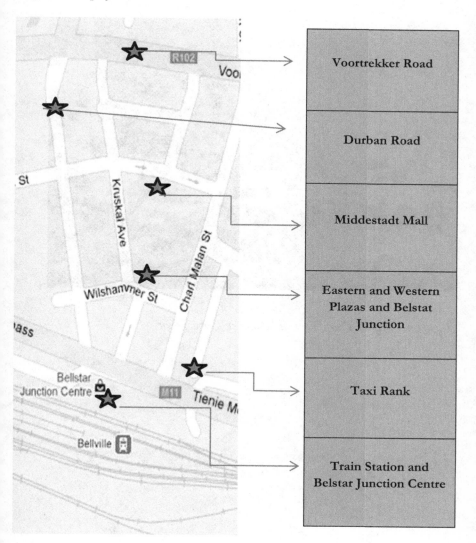

Figure 3: Wilshammer Street, Connecting the Main Roads

Figure 4: Map of Train Transit Routes in Cape Town

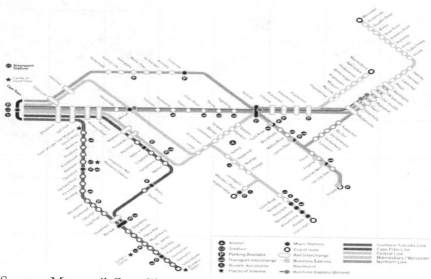

Source: Metrorail Cape Town

1. 2 Theorizing Conviviality: In Attempts to Understand the Convivial

If a reading of the literature is anything to go by, conviviality rests on the nuances imbibed in everyday relations - the micro-trends of socialization. The nature of a study about conviviality involves a study of society and its interrelations with sociality, diversity and social tensions and notions of space, place, citizenship and belonging. It is an investigation into styles of relating, of sociability and of how communality emerges from a negotiation of the constructive and the destructive. Conviviality may emerge from a resolution of frictions which, when turned into meaningful relationships, may actually facilitate mutual interests. These themes may emerge through a balance of positive and negative characteristics, humour and generosity versus coercion and anger, for example. Conviviality rests upon a foundation of neutrality, but is upheld by a brimming of aspirations, potentiality and pride. There is a shared imperative for harmony in convivial society. Maintained by a suppression of animosity, a convivial society may be seen as comprised of "amiable, intimate sets of relationships which carry, as well, a notion of peace and equality" (Overing and Passes, 2000: 14). Conviviality stresses empowerment for individuals and groups alike, and not the marginalization of the one by or for the other. Encouraging a convivial society may involve negotiating between different or competing agentive forces (Nyamnjoh, 2002: 111).

Conviviality is also related to the experience of space which is linked to sensory feelings and reactions that occur within a common place. Theoretical consideration of Bellville as a place of conviviality should be grounded in "having been there" with a consideration of culture as performance. "Culture as performance" implies the notion of culture as constructed and enacted through social relationships. It carries a connotation of intentionality and has often been linked to the assumption that cultural practices are intrinsically communicative (Harvey, 1996: 31). "Culture as performance" also leads us to consider Bourdieu's notion of habitus, or the embodiment of social norms, understandings and patterns of behaviour in individual actors (Hillier and Rooksby, 2005: 21). Habitus, which is expressed by the individual as an active and contributing member of society, is "constantly subjected to experiences, and therefore, constantly affected by them in a way that either reinforces or modifies its structures" (Hillier and Rooksby, 2005: 21). Furthermore, habitus is a product and producer of history. It produces individual and collective practices that are formed from a history of practices and which in turn become a history of practices. Habitus "ensures the active presence of past experiences, which, deposit in each organism in the form of schemes of perception, thought and action, tend to guarantee the 'correctness' of practices and their constancy over time" (Bourdieu, 1990: 54).

Habitus is the product of a history of social interactions, and is, therefore, a critical factor in the cognitive and embodied sense of place in Bellville. As an embodiment of history, incorporated habitus structures the daily life of those who possess it (Bourdieu, 1990: 56; Nyamnjoh, 2002: 114). We may theorize that the notion of habitus in Bellville is reflective of mobility, as experiences of migration and travel influence how individuals negotiate with diversity and shared space to inform their daily practices. Habitus is durable in Bellville but not immutable, influenced by a "field" of social space in which cultural performance takes place. It is, therefore, critical in an analysis of conviviality in Bellville, as it informs the extent to which individuals become – or have the potential to become - convivial towards each other as well as how the notion of "place" in Bellville is supportive of collective conviviality. If habitus is conceived of in terms of the metaphor of a "game", it is not just about the rules, but having a sense of the field, which requires awareness, alertness, responsiveness, flexibility and improvisation. It requires an assessment of team mates and opponents, and their strengths, weaknesses and intentions (Hillier and Rooksby, 2005: 23). The field may be a space of conflict and competition as people struggle to meet their own personal objectives and to define one's place and other's spaces. These notions define the collectivity of space and the nature of conviviality in place. As the analogy of a game demonstrates, conviviality may be a difficult force to maintain, requiring vigilance and even suffering in order to collectively deter negativity.

Inherent in the idea of place is the grounding of collective ideas – the convergence and emergence of qualities at a given historical time, leading to degrees of conviviality or contestation. Foucault's concept of "heterotopic spaces" – places where differences meet, where forms of collective life and collective experiences of otherness take shape – is relevant to an analysis of the spatial dimensions of conviviality amongst Bellville's migrant community (Foucault, 2007). This leads us to consider that personal sense of space in Bellville rests on a rhythm of deeply engrained practices (Ross, 2010: 66), which animate and give personal meaning to particular social places. Henri Lefebvre (2004) argues that rhythm, spatiality and temporality are intimately linked. He writes, "Everywhere there is an interaction between a place, a time and an expenditure of energy, there is rhythm" (2004: xv). Furthermore, "Rhythm is always linked to such and such a place" (2004, 89). The rhythm of daily life, though easily taken for granted, emphasizes the ways in which people resignify the meanings that their social environment affords to them (Harvey, 1996: 139). The outcomes of this research on conviviality and belonging further demonstrate how theoretical and ethnographic techniques in anthropology, such as the use of narrative to explore the rhythm of social life, inform understandings of space and place. By focusing on details of how local communities construct perceptions of place, experience place and further theorize about lived spaces and places, the nuances of daily life are revealed in ways that we may not ordinarily consider.

Understanding the diverse social context of Bellville, and what upholds its conviviality, requires an understanding of individual agency, that is, people and things as acting, reflecting moral agents. Society and sociality are mutually constructive, but both are based on the individual as a powerful agent, able to manipulate and build communities in space. Space offers a realm for the exercising of agency and the individual has the power to animate space to make it a place of particular interactions, therefore contributing to the collective meaning of place. Bellville as a social and political place reflects an on-going and continuous composition of different meanings, thoughts and judgements associated with the personal experience and deflection of space. While we share collective physical space, our concepts of place, of the meaning of those spaces, may differ. The concept of "place" is inherently personal, defined by experiences of space that create meaningful places of association. As Low and Lawrence-Zuniga (2003) demonstrate, it is the feelings that activities in different spaces evoke that make them places. As a result, some spaces may become more evocative than others, depending on how people have chosen to use space. The adaptability and flexibility of social space indicate the myriad of possibilities for its use, which may, intentionally or not, yield to forms of conviviality (Frank and Stevens, 2007).

1. 3 The Anthropological Concern: Why Study Conviviality in Bellville?

Anthropologist Arturo Escobar highlights that scholarship has tended to de-emphasize place and to instead highlight global trends and transnational flows, resulting in an, oftentimes, asymmetrical analysis with far too little value given to "place" (2008: 7). There is, therefore, a need to neutralize this erasure of "place" through a focus on the roles of space and place in locality. Further, in terms of studies on diversity in African cities, scholars have all too often focused on ethnic conflict and the emergence of nativist sentiments, on violent clashes that are fought over social and political difference. In many ways, these studies propagate a discourse of difference by relying on analytical categories that dichotomize social groups. In the context of globalization, increasing urban mobility, and rapidly transforming communities where almost everyone has been geographically and socially displaced, there is a need to encourage a greater research focus on the emergence of cosmopolitanism, multiculturalism and conviviality within the dynamics of space and place (Landau, 2011a:

14). In order to address questions of diversity in a post-migration context, it is further necessary to de-essentialize ethnicity as an analytical category. This is achievable through a focus on social cohesion and conviviality (Baumann and Sunier, 1995: 4). Analysis of these concepts is particularly revealing of the micro-level politics that foster both social relations (whether convivial or not) and conflict to define the dynamics of multiculturalism and how it emerges at a local level.

1. 4 Reflections on the Criticality of Bellville

I have reflected upon the Bellville CBD as a place of spatial and social transformation that is characterized by rapid movements out, in and through (Landau, 2011b: 2). The Bellville CBD is constantly being socialized by its long-term community, embedded culture, and passers-through, as they manoeuvre space and physically and imaginatively negotiate their relative positions. The very nature of being in a common space forces a (said or unsaid) relationship amongst the people, thus giving political, social and moral meaning to the place. However, as Landau writes, "The expansion and diversification of (South Africa's) urban centres are also generating new social relationships and patterns of conflict, poverty, and violence that often contrast the aspirations outlined by the country's inclusive Constitution. The 2008 'xenophobic' attacks are but the most extreme example" (Landau, 2011b: 2). Xenophobic violence of recent years has led to a collective memory of violence and intolerance towards foreigners in South Africa. As a result, migrants have become particularly vulnerable to violence, racism and violations of economic social, cultural, civil and political rights (SANPAD, 2011). Outsiders, both obvious and discreet, have increasingly come to be understood as a threat to the possibilities for retribution after years of Apartheid injustice (Landau, 2011a: 3), leading to the increasing manifestation of "blamocrats" (Farah, 2000: 188). Reactionary forces are eager to cash in on dynamics of social change, placing the blame in order to "pose as legitimate champions

11

of the interests of their unsettled nationals or ethnic kin" (Nyamnjoh 2006a: 228). The Bellville CBD has likely developed very different meaning in past years since the break-out of xenophobic violence throughout the Western Cape and the greater South Africa. Despite sharing the same physical space that previous populations and through-passers had inhabited and explored at Bellville train station and surrounds, local residents today occupy a very different place there, given such recent negative sentiments towards migrants. Violence exacerbates social distance and identifies group boundaries. It is in this context that social space becomes embedded in physical place (Jayaram, 2009), both of which form the basis for a study of conviviality.

1. 5 Mapping the Way–Direction Bellville

This ethnography draws on key concepts of space, place, mobility and being to address the emergence of conviviality in Bellville's central business district. The following chapter (Chapter 2) introduces the reader to the lived reality and everyday consciousness of the Bellville CBD. Its use of elements of "thick description" (Geertz, 1973) demonstrates how participant observation and narrative techniques may be significant methodological gateways to meaning-making about conviviality. Chapter 2 explores my approaches to an ethnographic study of Bellville – a diverse locality that yields opportunities, challenges and the inevitability of multivariable encounters. It also presents reflections about methodological and ethical considerations related to engaging in ethnographic practice in urban public space.

Chapter 3 addresses the structural, administrative and legal barriers to social inclusion for migrants, arguing that conviviality emerges in Bellville in the wider context of forced migration. A core aim of this book is to address the role of the state, of institutions and of the political economy as indicators of why Bellville has become a place of diversity for national and non-national migrants. Chapter 4 reflects on the narrative outcomes of state and public attitudes towards non-nationals. It further addresses the micro-sociological characteristics of conviviality in Bellville through narratives that reveal what it means to belong; social, family and business networks; the negotiation of physical space and methods of maintaining self-protection while on a journey into the unknown. It seeks to demonstrate how conviviality emerges from social relations in Bellville, contemplating how local dynamics of space and place play a critical role in its configurations.

Chapter 5 involves an interrogation of the nation-state-based model for citizenship, which is analysed in the context of trends towards mobility, xenophobia and autochthony. Bellville represents a place where spaces of globality meet spaces of territoriality. As such, it is a liminal zone where belonging is contested, is influenced by, and equally representative itself, of trends towards autochthony. Networks of mobility in Bellville, such as ICT infrastructures, the internet and the train station, build the backbone for a cosmopolitan society. At the same time, dynamics of flows are met with dialectics of immobility, characterized by strained social relations between nationals and non-nationals in South Africa. As such, this chapter interrogates modern understandings of citizenship – its root in the nation-state and its discursive embodiment in particular notions of rights represent the framework for urban inclusion, exclusion and degrees of conviviality.

As an ethnographic study of place, this book seeks to connect observations of space and place in Bellville to the context of increasing mobility, autochthony and violence against foreigners in South Africa's urban spaces. The expansion and diversification of Bellville has generated new social relationships formed out of mobilities that are met by forces of exclusion. Mobility, as an emerging global trend, manifests in urban space through flux, rebirth and negotiated meanings of place. As such, negotiations over space, place, citizenship and belonging are reflected in physical spaces of mobility; and convivial encounters are shaped by unique spatial settings and urban forms in Bellville.

2

Exploring "Somaliville"

This chapter aims to address the research methods used in this study, the issues that emerged in the field, and the ethical considerations that form the foundations of the research. These are addressed in the context of "doing" ethnography to explore how theorizing about ethnographic practice and practicing ethnography manifest different research expectations and outcomes. This chapter addresses why I decided to research Bellville, how I approached an ethnographic study of Bellville and key findings that contribute to a theorizing about ethnographic practice.

I decided to focus my fieldwork at the Bellville train station and surrounding central business district area after the excitement of my first field visit there. The train station reminded me of places I have been before and triggered memories of association — such as the flurry of being at the New Delhi or Nairobi stations. Every single person that I spoke to asked me where I am from, which led me to question notions of identity and belonging in Bellville. This is a question that I grapple to answer - having moved around globally to different places for so much of my life, I feel that I am both between places and amongst many; home is the world around me. My own social location is largely defined by my past travel experiences and relations with others in various parts of the world. Being amongst people in Bellville who have travelled, migrated and experienced many worlds, I think the real (or imagined) idea of "home" is a topic that we can deeply relate on, as knowledge gained from experiences during our "past lives" intertwines with our present. As an anthropologist, I am interested in reflecting on how concepts of belonging, home and community manifest figuratively through narratives, aesthetically, and in our roles as participants and producers of culture.

The central business district of Bellville is situated at a place where the new and the old South Africa meet, making it a suitable place to explore notions of multiculturalism and conviviality in public space. Monolithic beige buildings reminiscent of Apartheid era government structures stand parallel to a bustling marketplace filled with Valentine's Day singing bears, mannequins in bright yellow, green and red jeans, and buildings such as Wonderful Plaza where a diversity of people interact daily. It is a place where Afrikaans women now in their late 30s remarked, "We used to take the train to Bellville and hang around after school"; and where nowadays, little girls in dark coloured hijabs and pink sunglasses balanced atop on their heads stroll hand in hand with moms attending to daily errands. It is a place where a school bus – an initiative organized by the community – now drops Somali children home from school; they tease each other as they hop out onto the road, their colossal backpacks bouncing up and down as they stroll. It is a place that fifteen years ago many people from Bellville and other parts of Cape Town considered to have reached a point of being "inhabitable", filled with *skollies,* petty crime and drugs. However, in the past twenty years, migrants, and Somalis in particular, have recognized Bellville as a place brimming with opportunity, and have eagerly ensembled a marketplace for the masses. In many ways, the area has become gentrified due to the entrepreneurial vigour of transnational migrants, whose relationships with a polyglot city like Cape Town have led them to create a social enclave of their own. As populations accommodated by the area shift over time, the space imbibes new and different symbolic meanings.

Figure 5: Contrasting Durban Road through Imagery

2. 1. My Methods and Experiences of Meaning-Making

Ethnography allows for acute observation of the everyday through lived experiences that are interpreted to elicit social meaning. To quote Marcel Mauss (cited in Ferguson 1999: 17), "Ethnography is like fishing; all you need is a net to swing; and you will be sure to catching something." This metaphor resonates with me, as it describes the changes that occurred in my understanding of ethnographic research. Rather than directing the research, I found that I was best suited to letting go of expectations and participating and observing my surroundings with full attention. My approaches changed drastically, as I recycled pages of pre-mediated questions. In retrospect I understand that such an approach would not have elicited the nuances of conviviality that bring to light this ethnography of Bellville. Establishing relationships of trust and mutuality was of first and foremost importance. As such, I have come to know people in the field as most urbanites may know each other: some quite well, some only in passing, some through Facebook, and several others much more in-depth, which gave me detailed knowledge of various areas of their lives. "Deep hanging out" (Geertz, 2000: 110) and forming mutual relationships built off of trust were primary research "techniques", and hanging out allowed me to experience the true conviviality of people and place.

My research left me with a terrific sense of optimism – an optimism that during the course of my fieldwork was sometimes doubted due to stories of violence, denial of human rights and the hardships experienced by people in their active determination to succeed. The risks and adversities endured by many of the research participants, particularly those who have migrated in order to better support family far away; the liminal periods of trial and error and persistence despite shattered expectations of South Africa often left me empathetic and sad. However, despair, panic and fear did not emerge as characteristic of this research. Instead, the people that I met during my journey are overwhelmingly joyous, joking and friendly. They are wise and analytical of experiences of migration in South Africa, perhaps in order to make some sense of them. Such is the nature of conviviality, as it emerges from recognition of destruction and a conscious effort to positively reconstruct.

"Partnership" of Field Sites

My field research was scattered in time, extending between June and November of 2012. I also continued to engage with the field during the period of my writing and analysis from January to March 2013. It was beneficial to extend the research over several months of time, rather than to condense it into consecutive weeks, as this allowed me to develop deep and meaningful relationships with participants in a way that did not capitalize on their time. My research took motion as I became more socialized and familiar with the field, which extended to include various locations in and around the Bellville train station and central business district. Fieldwork took place at different times of the day and week and in various fluid contexts that are distinct but melt together (e. g. in the general space encompassed by the train/bus station, amongst different people who share space but have different experiences of it). In order to better understand the nature of conviviality in Bellville, I engaged with

19

several ethnographic techniques, which included narrative interview; participant observation; focus group discussion and data collection from secondary sources such as the media, official reports, scholarly books and articles as well as several novels and memoirs. Narrative inquiry through interviews and chatting was the primary method used to elicit meaningful information about people's social worlds at Bellville train station and central business district. I aspired towards Geertz's (1973) metaphor of "thick description" in collecting my field notes for interpretative ethnographic writing.

I proceeded with this research in the way that I hope it will be utilized in future – in partnership. I aimed to work in partnership with academic networks, with service providers who work selflessly towards providing critical services to refugees and migrants, with local advocacy channels such as the Somali Association of South Africa, and utmost importantly, with those whose stories bring life to these words. While the Bellville CBD was the main site of focus for this research, fieldwork took place in two distinct places. The first site was in Bellville itself and involved engaging with local residents and shopkeepers as well as extensive participant observation. It is important to note that participant observation as a research technique involves a high level of attentiveness, requiring me to set aside ideas about how things 'should' be in order to find out how they actually are (or aren't) (Ross, 2010: 10). The nature of "community" in Bellville occurs in an infinite number of small instances, which encouraged me to step outside of conventional ways of seeing and engage as a participant observer (ibid). The second site for information gathering was at a non-governmental organization that provides advocacy support, social services and a network based community for refugees in Cape Town. I volunteered there over the course of a year by teaching weekly English as a second language classes to a group of 30 students. Working as a teacher and advocate for refugee rights was an integral part of the research methodology, as it allowed me to build intimate relationships with students who face many similar issues to their peers in Bellville. It also increased my exposure to people willing to participate in research, thus assisting towards a snowball sampling approach, as many students were well connected with Bellville residents and associations, or were from Bellville themselves.

I also developed close and meaningful relationships with various local community based organizations, such as the Somali Association of South Africa. Through these connections I was able become active outside of my research role by volunteering, which enabled me to participate and observe the development of organizational goals and achievement of outcomes. For example, during the course of my research, The Somali Association of South Africa opened the Bellville Education Centre, an English language school that will ideally assist students in Bellville to learn English for social and business involvements, encouraging social cohesion and conviviality. It was inspiring to see community-driven initiatives such as these manifest from aspirations and ideas into living operations with a network of administrators, volunteers and participants who represent the future for local governance and social cohesion in Bellville. I hope that this research will provide a critical research and advocacy tool for various implementing partners to further common goals and objectives. It may, for instance, be used in future years as a baseline to understand how dynamics of conviviality and social cohesion may have changed.

Narrative Techniques

This book aims to reveal how mobility and conviviality in Bellville are represented by *emotional* beings whose lives, histories and intentions are best understood through narrative ethnography. It answers to the call for conceptual flexibility and ethnographic substantiation (Nyamnjoh, 2013) by looking beyond academic sources - to include narrative fiction and personal memoirs – as ways of understanding deeply personal and emotive experiences of being. Ethnography succeeds in narrating the everyday, thereby mitigating the empirical nature of so-called social scientific studies in which subjects are often represented as research subjects rather than characters with personalities, feelings and personal and social beliefs (Nyamnjoh and Brudvig, 2013: 8). It is through use of narrative

21

techniques that the experience of belonging in the everyday becomes compassionately studied through vivid account. As such, this book seeks to portray a deep, flexible and nuanced understanding of mobility and social interconnections in Bellville, acknowledging that the locality is situated within a world that is permanently on the move (Nyamnjoh, 2013).

My use of narrative based techniques involved engaging with participants about their daily involvements in and around Bellville, significant events and people that they interact with, as well as anecdotes about everyday life and local and international politics. If participants seemed willing to open up further, I continued to develop conversation which allowed participants to be comfortable enough to talk about memories, life stories and personal opinions. In this sense, research themes developed using a snowball approach based on how participants conjure meaning and how willing they became to developing a relationship. Important considerations in using narrative included the methods of storytelling, the process of self-reflection and the meaning that is ascribed to words and emotions through storytelling. Narratives inherently contain people's perceptions and, often, their own interpretations of meaning derived from lived realities. They also contain the interpretation of the receiver, whose own understanding of the narrative may be influenced by their particular social world; a situation further complicated by field realities of translation from or into the language of the researcher or the interlocutor. Interviewing, transcription, coding and analysis rely on very different factors of interpretation. As James Scheurich writes, "Interviewing as a research method can be artificially separated into two parts. The first part is actually doing the interview; the second is interpreting the interview" (Scheurich, 1997: 61). It is because of these layers of interpretation and recount that narratives are a valuable technique in attempting to understand social worlds, life histories and current experiences of being. Through these stages, I was able to develop a closer understanding about myself as an ethnographer, including my interpretation of narratives and worlds.

22

Participant Observation

In addition to collecting personal narratives, participant observation was an integral method to understanding notions of conviviality, belonging and negotiations with space in the Bellville CBD. The micro-politics of daily life were often best nuanced through this technique and it allowed for an interpretive approach in analysis (Geertz, 1978). From a research perspective, participant observation required me to treat many seemingly incidental aspects of daily life as important to the micro-politics of conviviality (Block, 2009: 9). Participant observation also evoked the possibility to explore the counter narrative. In some cases, direct observations debunked myths and assumptions and contrasted with verbal narrative. Prolonged participant observation of people's movement, encounters and reactions, interactions and language (including body language) was a valuable technique to understand arising emotions, sociability and movement in space. I observed particularly interesting ways of communicating, such as vendors repeatedly advertising a product over his microphone loudspeaker ("1 kg of yogurt for R11. 99") and music in different languages being reproduced and played in shops; both of these examples draw meaning about social interaction. Music is representative of degrees of musical conviviality and cacophony, providing a metaphor for social conviviality in Bellville that will be explored in Vignette 5.

Participant observation in Bellville also involved self-reflection, in other words, a reflexivity of my own presence in the area and the impact of my social role. As Michel de Certeau (1988) argues, a reading of social space has much to do with one's own position in it. In researching conviviality, a certain neighbourly-ness is necessary in order to become a convivial participant in society. Being convivial enabled me to observe both my own and others' reactions. Further, in order to work effectively in the field, the anthropologist must establish a plausible role within the community to establish trust (Appadurai, 2003). In some cases I was a facilitator for giving directions or translating business transactions, in other times a shopper, and in many times, a direct and honest researcher, pen and

23

paper in hand. This is reflective of George Marcus's idea that, "The condition of shifting personal position in relation to one's subjects and other active discourses in a field that overlap with one's own generates a definite sense of doing more than just ethnography, and it is this quality that provides a sense of being an activist" (1995: 113). My own relation to the field led me to become an ethnographer come "circumstantial activist" (ibid).

My method in participant observation took into consideration Gupta and Ferguson's challenge to the idea of bounded culture; that is, "the idea that 'a culture' is naturally the property of a spatially localized people and that the way to study such a culture is to go 'there'" (Gupta & Ferguson, 1997: 3). After meeting several residents or frequenters of Bellville's central business district, several of our interviews, and by extension my observation of or introduction to some of the other contexts that mattered in their lives, took place outside of Bellville. This was often dependent upon the daily schedule of participants who often transit in and out of Bellville. I also was able to investigate the "culture" of Bellville independent of the defined spatial locality by reaffirming my observations of Bellville with students at the NGO and with leaders of community based organizations working in Bellville. Since Bellville is a place of transit, it was necessary to challenge the notion of bounded culture, which was achieved by gathering a variety of perspectives from people within and outside of the field site before drawing conclusions. Thus, I have aimed to "turn away from the common sense idea that such things as locality and community are simply given or natural and turn toward a focus on social and political processes of place making, conceived less as a matter of 'ideas' than of embodied practices that shape identities" (Gupta & Ferguson, 1997: 4).

This study of space, place and conviviality also included participatory mapping of the area with the aim of understanding spatial, social, and possibly object-related, relationships, networks and interactions. The spatial dynamics of belonging that emerged from this exercise were of great importance and provided a critical point of reflection for me in my research. In mapping the area with a local resident, Charles, the barriers of his map were narrow and confined to particular avenues within the field site. It was almost as if there emerged an invisible line nearby the taxi rank, which several residents that I have liaised with seem hesitant to cross. This outcome is explored later in Section 4. 6 as an analysis of "insiders" and "outsiders" in Bellville's central business district.

Focus Group Discussion

I held several focus group discussions as part of the research methodology, including one at the NGO amongst students and one at a meeting of civil society stakeholders. The purpose of these discussions was to explore grand and theoretical perspectives of diversity, culture, local communities, governance and sociality. Discussions included themes such as the difficulties encountered by migrants and refugees in South Africa (and Bellville) and assumed reasons for such problems, social integration, and the need to remain unified within the non-national and diaspora communities of South Africa. These discussions were integral to establishing, through participatory methods, the theoretical frameworks for key analytical terms such as "culture", "religion" and "social integration". In a discussion about the role of religion, language and culture in cultural assimilation, participants emphasized that "religion is an issue of spirit, it is about faith. But culture, this is different. It is not about attitudes, language, behaviour like everyone says. It is about the way we do things." Another participant noted, "You can change behaviour, but you cannot change attitude, therefore, attitude is personal and therefore not a part of culture, which is about a group identity." A valuable conclusive statement to the discussion was, "Our differences should not be discussed in term of cultural difference, but lifestyle difference, for we all practice common traditions." These discussions provided significant analytical content that helped me to situate myself in Bellville's narrative worlds.

2. 2 Ethical Considerations

I continuously reflected on ethical considerations and potential outcomes that arise in research practice. Additionally, I sought out various pieces of literature on the ethics and challenges of constructing ethical relationships when working with refugees, as there is a large refugee community amongst migrants in Bellville. This literature addresses "the difficulties in constructing an ethical consent process and obtaining *genuinely* informed consent" (Mackenzie, McDowell, Pittaway, 2007: 300). During the course of my field research I made sure to maintain full transparency in my research goals and intentions. I did this by asking each participant that I interacted with to provide verbal informed consent with the option of maintaining confidentiality/anonymity throughout the study. The extent to which I used the information provided by the participant was negotiated with the participant and their reflections were respected. In most cases, I decided to keep individuals anonymous unless they truly reflected *genuine* verbal and emotional consent for their names to be included. This involved a reflection about the extent to which it was really necessary to include named identities in the research. I was also conscious to remain alert for situations where a participant may decide to withdraw consent. Protecting and maintaining a respectful and equal relationship amongst community members and research informants remained my mantra.

I also remained continuously conscious of my own social role in the community, and particularly my gendered role, to consider who I associated with, interacted with and the methods that I used. Additionally, the research ran the risk that relationships amongst community members may not be convivial, in which case I was cautious about my role in terms of it affecting some aspect of community relations, depending on whom I associated with. Likewise, interviewing a police officer in public or in the presence of others may have made people more sceptical of information that they provide me, knowing that I had liaised with the police. My interactions, therefore, had to be very nuanced and diplomatic.[1] In some cases individuals were hesitant to engage in research-related activities. They may have felt that they needed to protect themselves from "outsiders" such as myself. They may have been sceptical to provide certain information related to their relationship with South African authorities such as the Department of Home Affairs, for example. This dilemma evokes James Scheurich's postmodern critique of research interviewing. This perspective suggests that "the researcher has multiple intentions and desires, some of which are consciously known and some of which are not. The same is true of the interviewee" (Scheurich, James, 1997: 62). In cases where the intentions and desires to participate were unclear, I did not probe and instead interviewed others.

Methodological and analytical outcomes of my research also incite the ethical dilemma presented by Ferguson and Gupta who write, "How can 'we' anthropologists presume to speak for 'them' our informants? Is not 'our' knowledge of 'them' inevitably shaped by colonial and neo-colonial power relations that render the whole enterprise suspect? How can 'our' anthropological mission of understanding 'others' proceed without falling into the familiar traps of exoticization, primitivism and orientalism?" (2001: 24). Anthropologists participate in the "politics of representation" through research on communities and individuals. Therefore, my ethical considerations involved taking ethnographic methods as a form of political practice. Ethically, this involved maintaining a "predicament-oriented approach" (Nyamnjoh, 2007b). Reflexivity in the field remained critical to "recognizing a variety of different ways in which anthropological representations may be engaged with questions of culture and power, place making and people making, resistance and subjectivity (Ferguson and Gupta, 2001: 24-5), and to understanding that "knowledge *of* people grants power *over* people" (Nyamnjoh, 2007b: 6).

---

[1] I have purposely excluded my direct observations of police activities, but do reflect upon the role of government authorities in Section 3.

I believe that it is impossible to do full justice to my research questions, nor can I presume to understand my informants fully or to express their knowledge and experience through my word and world of knowledge. In this book I wish to avoid politicizing culture and identity and aim to yield my ethnographic authority to those whose narratives form the basis on this book. However, words themselves are forms of meaning-making, and despite my intentions, the political may be inevitable (Wright, 1998). I aim to maintain myself as a neutral figure of authority in this book by presenting direct quotations, interviews and vignettes to support my claims, by placing myself as a reflexive actor in narrative and by historicizing the context of migration in Bellville in Chapter 3. In terms of narrative analysis, such as that which forms the body of Chapter 4, I aim to portray a snapshot of my interpretation of daily life. This ethnography is loyal to James Clifford's concept of "partial truths", in which a rigorous sense of partiality contributes to the writing of "true fiction" (Clifford, 1986: 5). Ethical considerations have led me to question the extent to which ethnography is more about the subject or the writer. I have concluded that ethnography – anthropological research – has a life of its own.

2. 3 Of Pavements and Pathways; Networks and Neighbours

This chapter demonstrates how structure in ethnographic research can be a hindrance, as ethnographic research is driven and derived by nuances. It is based upon the chance for experience, in which case research outcomes may be described as lived experiences themselves. Sparking rich conversation with Bellville residents, initiating convivial gestures and negotiating my relationship with "their" space through trial and error continuously crafted my personal style of research within the methods of participant observation, mapping and narrative dialogue. As Lesley Green writes, "In fieldwork, one is never simply interviewing or observing – one is working with oneself, from oneself, in a relationship with others. In ethnography, the surface of learning is you, your body, your experience, and your ability to be a comfortable presence on the stranger's threshold" (Green, 2008: 2). While I initially set out with my proposal and research goals in mind, I soon realized that I would gather greater insight about conviviality in Bellville not by looking for it, but by participating, "hanging out" and going about usual tasks there; reacting and thriving off of the issues that present themselves in daily life. In conclusion, I have realized that intuition, exploration and interpretation are all equally valuable to ethnographic research, and particularly so in urban public spaces where channels, networks and embodied meanings are often learned through lived experiences amongst convivial strangers.

3

Social Histories of Migration

Conviviality emerges in Bellville in the wider context of forced migration. This chapter sets out to situate Bellville as place that has become embroiled in the international politics of refugee protection and global human rights discourse. It seeks to answer the question of "why Bellville?" in terms of international conventions towards the protection of refugees in order to question the extent to which South Africa's commitment to refugees holds strong. The institutional, legal and administrative barriers in negotiating refugee status and receiving protection in South Africa today form a significant role in configurations of rights and recognition of rights in communities of diversity and mobility such as Bellville (SANPAD, 2011). The personal outcomes of these barriers, which may be described of as barriers to rights, contribute to how migrants relate to urban public space - critical to analysis on how meaning is attributed to space and place in Bellville as well as the dynamics of conviviality that emerge. Conviviality, therefore, emerges from a great deal of negotiation by individuals and communities at both the micro and macro levels (Nyamnjoh, 2002: 135). While some migrants in Bellville may have welcomed the excitement of new experiences and transitions, such as Charles who left Tanzania on an adventurous streak with ambitions to travel, others, such as many Somali migrants, may have been forced to flee home and arrived as refugees. This chapter seeks to deconstruct narrative experiences of barriers to rights that both Charles and his Somali neighbours face by contextualizing the institutional, legal and administrative context of forced migration into Bellville.

3. 1 Addressing South Africa's Reactions to Migrants through Narrative

South Africa has experienced a full spectrum of migration and displacement, transitioning from a refugee/migrant "producing" country to a "receiving" country, in terms of cross-border migration. South Africa currently has the highest number of asylum seekers in the world (HRW, 2011). Since South Africa's immigration framework provides little opportunity for legal migration from other African countries, economic migrants have turned to the country's asylum system in overwhelming numbers. Demand on the system exceeds its functionality and inconsistencies in immigration policy have hindered the effectiveness of the refugee system in South Africa. As a result, the protective nature of the refugee system has been transformed into one of control – motivated by the need to reduce the influx of economic migrants (Amit, 2011: 458).

Many non-national asylum seekers and refugees in Bellville entered South Africa with the assumption, or perhaps just hope, that they would receive international protection under the conditions of the refugee regime to which South Africa is party. However, Georgina, a Congolese woman who works on hair braiding in Bellville, explained in our conversation about the refugee reception centre in Cape Town, "You can't believe that they can treat people like this here." She continued. "People stand there in lines, maybe they are trying to get their documents but while they wait through this process, they don't have them, so maybe they are taken to prison. At the previous reception centre (in Nyanga) it was very bad, maybe they would be shot for being a foreigner." Such stories reflect the lived experiences that emerge from domestic policies and protocols and global conventions towards migrants and refugees.

Narrative and ethnography contextualize the lived experience of migration. The experience of migration, and forced migration in particular, encompasses extraordinarily diverse historical and political causes. Those who have been forced to migrate embody qualitatively different situations and predicaments – their habitus is unique despite sharing varied experiences of displacement. As Malkki notes, "The term 'refugee' has analytical usefulness not as a label for a special, generalizable 'kind' or 'type' of person or situation, but only as a broad legal or descriptive rubric" (Malkki, 1995: 496) – in which case narrative becomes a critical technique in order to understand individual experiences of being. Narrative methods further demonstrate how national commitments are translated into practice and how conventions become interpreted and implemented by the state. Ethnography, in particular, reveals the hardship that refugees experience through encounters with the South African state.

3. 2 "In Bellville, you see, many of us are refugees"

This section draws on South Africa's refugee policy, as well as the implementation of it through legal and administrative structures, to demonstrate the inadequacies of the international refugee protection regime and what this means for a majority of residents in Bellville who are Somali refugees. The international refugee protection conventions, consisting of the 1951 and 1967 Conventions and the United Nations High Commission for Refugees (UNHCR) mandate, are intended to secure refugee protection and rights, however, the challenges of accessing these demonstrate the trials and tribulations of institutionalizing human rights. In today's world of international relations, states guard their moral identities and commitments to human rights by falling back on their signature to key documents, frameworks, protocols. However, these documents have become mere instruments of the state (Loescher, 2003: 6). The manner in which states integrate refugee rights into domestic policy – and the extent to which bureaucracy enables for administrative access to stated rights – demonstrates not only the extent of state commitments to human rights, but the extent to which they are committed to supporting cultural diversity with a hospitable civic order, a critical trajectory for cosmopolitanism and liberal democratic state identity (Gilroy, 2005: 2). This has further implications for notions of citizenship as will be explored later in this book.

The international refugee protection regime consists of the 1951 UN Convention Relating to the Status of Refugees, the 1967 Protocol and the United Nations High Commission for Refugees (UNHCR) mandate. The 1951 Convention was created in the aftermath of the Second World War and defined the boundaries of who is a refugee. According to this document, a refugee is someone who "has fled his or her home country owning to a well-founded fear of persecution" (Loescher, 2003: 3). The 1951 Convention's impetus for an international commitment to refugees was extended internationally through the 1967 Protocol. "The 1967 Protocol was significant in that it not only removed the time and geographical limitations from the definition of a refugee, but it also committed states to apply to protections contained in the 1951 Convention" (Copeland, 2003: 108). To respond to an ever-expanding refugee crisis – in which the number of global refugees grew enormously from about two million in 1951 to over 12 million at the beginning of the 21[st]century – the international community channelled assistance to refugees through UNHCR (Loescher, 2003: 3). Consequently, the organization became the centrepiece of global refugee protection.

While adoption of these frameworks by states should imply the sovereign prerogative for signatories to uphold commitments to refugees, this has not been the general trend. Instead, the concept of sovereignty is used by states such as South Africa as a protective weapon to guard against an influx of non-nationals. In South Africa, this has led to a crisis of increasing xenophobia at the state level, a political attitude that has filtered through society leading to widespread violence against non-nationals in past years. Responsibilities to refugees and asylum seekers are increasingly evaded by South Africa, despite being signatory to international conventions. The closure of critically located refugee offices in South Africa, the detention, deportation and criminalization of non-nationals, and the propagation of public xenophobic perspectives through the media are examples of how South Africa has internalized this trend and instigated a discourse of "insiders" and "outsiders". "A chain of transfer of responsibility" (De Jong, 1998: 692) and widespread denial of states to respect their responsibilities towards refugees signal that international refugee conventions have been interpreted in isolation of commitments to international human rights law. In South Africa the administrative failure that compounds legal proceedings has resulted in the maintenance of a state of perpetual liminality for many migrants, as their legal positioning and access to basic human rights are thwarted by periods of waiting. As Sutton et al. write, "Waiting…is a highly subjective emotion linked to endurance, hope, impatience and, for refugees facing the considerable threat of being an illegal immigrant who can be thrown out of the country, outright anger, fear and dread" (2011: 32). In practice, these processes (though intended to protect) only further incite fear of state institutions and of local society.

Evasion of South Africa's responsibilities to international conventions has been possible without legal consequence or significant international scrutiny due to the blurred definition of who is a refugee. Who is a refugee? The definition of a refugee as declared by the Convention is largely ambiguous. The Convention defines a refugee as anyone who:

> "Owing to a well-founded fear of being persecuted for reasons of race, religion, nationality, membership of a particular group or political opinion, is outside the country of his nationality and is unable or, owing to such fear, is unwilling to avail himself of the protection of that country"(UNHCR, 2006).

The refugee definition speaks directly to a post-World War II era (Steinbock, 1999: 18), one prior to our world of flows. The international refugee protection regime was introduced during East-West struggles between communism and capitalist democracy. The concept of an international framework for refugees was created in a very specific historic context that predates colonial resistance movements, independence from colonial rule, the postcolonial state and globalization (De Jong, 1998: 690). During the Cold War "refugees were perceived as *elements of power* in the bipolar rivalry"

(Loescher, 2003: 7). Fuelled by civil, religious and ethnic conflicts, as opposed to war across state borders, the nature of war and conflict today is very different from the context in which the refugee protection framework was created. The concept of a refugee does not correspond with the nature of war and persecution today, in which a majority of victims are internally displaced within the borders of their own countries. With major emergencies occurring simultaneously in Syria, South Sudan, Mali and the Democratic Republic of Congo, victims of internal wars are many (UNHCR, 2012). This creates a major dilemma, as internally displaced victims do not receive protection from international refugee law because they have not crossed a state border, and are thus not legally subject to international law.

Broad social categories included in the definition for reasons of persecution (e. g. race and religion) leave room for narrow interpretation of these concepts. As Steinbock states, "The text of the refugee definition constitutes what might be described as the boundary of its application" (Steinbock, 1999: 17). As Sztucki notes, "Today the *causes* and *context* of persecution have changed" (Sztucki, 1999: 60). A Kenyan woman in Bellville named Aayan perhaps illuminated better "who is a refugee" when she explained, "Somalis arrive on trucks, boats, walking. I arrived by plane to Joburg and then changed planes to Cape Town. They are asylum seekers; they don't have passports and so must be given refugee documents in order to protect them."

However, it is important to note that the fundamental barrier to accessing refugee rights is the way refugee status determination is handled. Currently, in order to access protection in a foreign country, asylum seekers must prove their "well-founded fear". The refugee definition does not acknowledge the fear of generalized fear that characterizes modern day conflicts. Furthermore, how can one prove fear? Becoming a refugee relies on being able to legitimize persecution at both personal and institutional levels, whereas shouldn't it be the case that "he does not become a refugee because of recognition, but is recognized because he is a refugee" (Smith,

2004: 53)? As Fiona Ross writes, self-disclosure asks us to assess the self, yet narrating one's life story may render one vulnerable to being mis-interpreted by the listener (2010: 143). Conveying a well-founded fear not only involves yielding to a Cerberean interpreter, but it is an intimate recall of pain. Nuruddin Farah recounts the psychological difficulties that this may evoke. He writes, "We dwell on past horrors in our remembering and concentrate our minds on the future's uncertainties, because we are afraid to face up to our sad fate" (2000: 18). Furthermore, a person may feel fear based on an event in the past or fear of the future. However, the problem here is that for "persecution to be *bad enough*, it has to be relatively recent" (Bohmer and Shuman, 2008: 181). *Imagine being told your pain is not bad enough?* Nuruddin further notes, "To flee a city in the siege of a strife...and then try to dock in a harbour where you're not welcome and where you are humiliated: this defines the sad state of a refugee's life" (2000, 78). To invoke commitments to international conventions and then question migrants as if in a criminal business make us consider that the terms "guest" and "host" are in fact, moral, not legal (Farah, 2000,172).

In the refugee application process the applicant must demonstrate that the government of his or her native country is responsible for persecution, though this depends on what states acknowledge as persecution over prosecution. This depends entirely on the culturally relative context of what is regarded as legitimate state practice. The fine line between prosecution and persecution is narrowed further in instances of internal state conflict, as transitioning regimes skew perceptions of government authority and create new targets (Bohner and Shumer, 2008: 182). Proving fear also poses literal challenges because victims of war may flee without documentation, or they may have been destroyed during their journey. Further, in explaining one's fear and need for protection, an asylum seeker may have difficulty expressing his or her experience in terms of political and legal terminology; this trouble is compounded for most asylum seekers who must communicate their story in another language. Applicants may not be able to read or write in the required language to the extent that the complexities of the forms demand, and translation services may not accurately portray personal experiences, due to the nature of translation. Gaining refugee status often depends on language skills, education, money for legal assistance, and ultimately, luck. The layers of bureaucracy inherent in this process represent "mechanisms of control" (Foucault 2007) used by the state for purposes of legitimization. In South Africa the administrative failure that compounds procedures has resulted in the maintenance of a state of perpetual liminality for many migrants, as their legal positioning and access to basic human rights are thwarted by periods of waiting.

On the other hand, the limitations of the refugee definition are also reflective of the agency migrants exercise in the face of "the boundaries of its application", as asylum seekers such as Daniel (see below) seek to manoeuvre the system by claiming refugee status by every means possible – including unauthorized ways, such as switching identities. While to some this may appear dishonest, one may further consider that it might simply be the only alternative to getting by. While the refugee definition stifles its protective capacity, migrants who fall in the face of its narrow interpretation may choose simply to not conform, opting instead to 'stick it out', despite shattered hopes and unclear expectations. Some may seek to manipulate structures in place, in which networks of social capital may provide useful channels to 'make a plan' when the going gets tough. By mediating with the truth of their circumstances, migrants negotiate the limits of their conviviality with the state and, in turn, create new channels that contribute to their social networks of micro-convivial encounters.

Vignette 1

Many refugees experience periods of perpetual liminality, characterized by waiting, endurance, fear and hope

Daniel is from Burundi and escaped because an outbreak of violence over land reform. His father was killed and Daniel feared for his life. He escaped to Kenya but struggled in Nairobi, a vicious city for refugees and the urban poor alike, and instead found his way to Mombasa where he was advised he could find work at the shipping dock. He heard about the possibility of hiding in a cargo ship and escaping, and when the opportunity came to become a hideaway on a ship en-route to America, Daniel jumped at the chance for refuge. He hid with some others in the basement of the ship, but was then discovered by a crew member. The ship would stop in South Africa, and Daniel was advised to disembark the ship and apply for refugee status. We met in Bellville.

Daniel disembarked the ship in early February 2012. He met several other migrants who gave him a bit of money for food and told him they can help to arrange accommodation for him. Upon arriving at the accommodation, Daniel was robbed at knife point and left with nothing but the clothes on his back. He was then imprisoned when he was found without legal documentation, as he was still waiting for the outcome of his refugee status application. While in prison, he exchanged refugee application reference numbers with someone, which allowed him to re-apply. He lived at a shelter for some time, but the costs were difficult to afford. He travelled often to the refugee centre to continue the process required of his application, which was successful several months later. He found a job working with heavy machinery that caused him injury in his leg, and he faced difficulty walking for a period of time. Vulnerable in this state, he was robbed one night at the train station, his temporary refugee papers and all of his money taken from him. Robbed of his identity, his legal standing in the country, his hope and his efforts to re-create a life far from Burundi - life became a walk of fear. He was nonetheless optimistic and courageous, an outcome of his fate.

3. 3 The Paradox of Protection

The refugee protection regime suffers from its own definition of a refugee, as it lacks coherency and leaves judgment at the discretion of the South African state. These issues speak to Harri Englund's suggestion, that the universalism of human rights is often sacrificed to "political expediency" (Englund, 2006: 47). Refugee protection is ideally a system of enabling access to justice. However, in South Africa, refugee "protection" has become a system of self-defence, a test of one's true limits of fear, as immigrants, refugees and asylum seekers are treated as criminals - scapegoated for crimes, punished for not having appropriate documentation (which itself is the fault of administrative failures of the government), and violently harassed when successful in long-term business goals. Creating a new life in South Africa as a refugee is a walk of fear. As Charles explained during my fieldwork in Bellville, "The police forget that we all have the right to live – they treat us as a criminal before having the chance to even just be a suspect." This situation further incites Giorgio Agamben's concept of *Homo Sacer* – in that the sovereign state (of exception) creates mechanisms through which human lives become the objects of political strategy, and therefore of a general strategy of power. Without access to full citizenship rights in any country – without a defined relationship with a state, "situated at the margins of the political order" (Agamben, 1995: 6) – asylum seekers may represent Agamben's concept of "bare life". Control of bare life through "mechanisms of control" (Foucault, 2007) represents the state's consolidation of "bio-power". By placing biological life at the centre of its controls, the modern state brings to light the secret tie uniting modern consolidations of power and bare life (Agamben, 1995: 5). The exceptional state of sovereignty and its power over "bare life" have tremendous significance to the relationship between refugees and the state, as well as the role that Bellville plays in accommodating needs for safety and protection in the absence of legal support.

The UNHCR, as a designated implementing agent for international refugee protection, is the single most important body for the protection of refugees, yet its reliance on state cooperation limits its capacity to pursue its mandate. In most countries, governments have yielded to international conventions and have abdicated responsibility of refugee status determination to the UNHCR, giving them full discretion to implement international refugee law domestically. In these situations, the UNHCR has the institutional leverage to negotiate administrative matters (e. g. documentation) with the government. In the context of South Africa, the government Department of Home Affairs controls this process[2], and thus, state sovereignty is the single biggest obstacle to refugee protection. Though the UNHCR is primarily a protection agency, state sovereignty has created barriers to the scope of protection that the organization can provide without "interfering" with domestic politics (Forsythe, 2001: 31). States that obstruct access are increasingly a problem, such as in Sudan, Somalia, and Myanmar. In these cases, the UNHCR must manoeuvre around state sovereignty to provide legal protection to refugees, and in doing so, concentrates on humanitarian assistance instead. This has led the UNHCR to become trapped in a protection-assistance dilemma, as its existence as a non-political actor limits its ability to respect the core of its protection mandate. The UNHCR, as the only *international* institution with the mandate conduct refugee status determination in the place of states, and thus to *implement* international commitments to refugee protection, remains trapped by its own foundations as a non-political actor whose role has a limited influence in the context of state rejection (Loescher et al, 2008: 104). As David Foesythe argues, the UNHCR has to appear very non-political in order to create space to pursue its goals of providing neutral care and protection to persons of concern (Forsythe, 2001: 2). In doing this, the UNHCR is, in fact, highly political in its actions, as its activities shift the dynamics of

---

[2]UNHCR does have presence in South Africa and relationships with several implementing partners that offer legal, social and administrative services.

power on local, regional, and global levels. Rather than a reminder of their responsibilities, states use sovereignty as a protective shield - to enforce their "exceptional state". The UNHCR must use the powers of persuasion, international law, and creative diplomacy to manoeuvre political space and create a presence in states that are increasingly irresponsible and impermeable (Forsythe, 2001: 15). The limited legal capacity of the UNHCR in South Africa, compounded by administrative delays and failures within the Department of Home Affairs, has led to dire consequences reflected in barriers to rights faced by migrants. This reflects poorly on South Africa's international commitments to refugee protection.

Several states have adopted "prima facie" policies where asylum seekers of a particular origin (of "refugee producing countries") are understood to be refugees due to regardless of the "truth" of their story. In South Africa, for instance, Somalis are considered as "prima facie" refugees, meaning that the mere notion of being Somali grants refugee status due to the political circumstances of Somalia. The notion of "prima facie" status stems from the 1969 Organization of African Unity (OAU) Convention, which specifies governing refugee jurisprudence and practice in Africa, and emerged in the context of decolonization (Handmaker et al., 2007). However, once Somali refugees go through initial entry administrative procedures - once they have a temporary refugee permit - it is near impossibly to access subsequent administration that is necessary for their longer-term protection and integration into South African society. One Somali man that I have come to know though my fieldwork in Bellville came to South Africa ten years ago as a refugee. After five years of living and working in South Africa, he was legally entitled to citizenship rights. He claimed, "I tried, over and over again, but the process does not move forward. I applied for a hearing with the Standing Committee, but there is no one to ask or blame, the process is stagnant. We have rights, but there is no one to help enforce them." Once granted refugee status, refugees are denied further support which often prevents them from accessing social services. They often face intolerance from local populations and are subjects to crime and harassment, even by the police who are often advantageous towards non-nationals. In South Africa this became a prominent national issue in 2008 with the outbreak of xenophobia violence. However, it is a daily reality for many, notable by the frequent looting of Somali shops and killing of shopkeepers across the country, amongst many other injustices. This situation has led many refugees in South Africa to live in fear, afraid to leave their apartments lest they are identified as a foreigner and interrogated by the police about their documentation or by a passerby about their looks.

One of my main liaisons in the field, Charles, spoke the importance of carrying around his passport at all times – he indicated to his breast pocket where it was kept and asked me if I have my ID with me. I had it in my purse. My conversation with Immortel, a man who considered himself a refugee from the DRC demonstrated the sense of insecurity and uncertainty that asylum seekers face in the institutional and administrative struggles to establish their rights as refugees.

In other regions of the world, administrative failure has led to the extension of "protracted refugee situations", where refugees are admitted for asylum and then "warehoused" in refugee camps for decades, denied their rights as set forth in the 1951 Convention (Feyissa and Horn, 2008: 23). However, the word "camp" does not appear in the text of the Convention (Smith, 2004). As Achille Mbembe writes, "the camp ceases to be a provisional place, a space of transit that is inhabited while awaiting a hypothetical return home. From the legal as well as the factual point of view, what was supposed to be an exception becomes routine and the rule within an organization of space that tends to become permanent" (Mbembe, 2000: 270). According to The South African Sunday Times in an article dated December 2, 2012, a discourse had re-risen amongst South African policy makers about the re-establishment of refugee camps (Jordan, 2012). This news was reported on after a significant period of contestation between civil society and the Department of Home Affairs about the closure of several critically located refugee reception centres.

Immortel: I can say something…everywhere you can go, the big problem is about papers in South Africa. It's not easy, they don't give us papers. I'm here …going on four years and I still have that paper, how do you call it…

Me: Which one?

Immortel: They gave it to me just for six months and I have to go back again after six months

Me: Oh did you go get it from Maitland?

Immortel: Yeah, but they are supposed to give us maybe two year and you can go back there, but they gave us six months.

Me: And what happens after six months, you have to go back and renew?

Immortel: Yes, but sometimes they don't give it to you. You have to pay sometimes money, it's not easy.

Me: Did they interview you?

Immortel: Yeah, already.

Me: And you didn't hear back?

Immortel: Nothing.

Me: About that interview, I'm curious…who was the person interviewing you?

Immortel: The first one was from South Africa and at that time I didn't know how to speak English. But he just write write, write, and I see some words…now when I understand I know that it said, he writes "mistake" in my paper.

Me: Because he doesn't understand you?

Immortel: Yes, he didn't understand what I was saying. The second time they gave me someone who speaks French and that was easy. They told me "you can wait, you are going to get your paper."

Me: But you didn't hear back.

Immortel: Nothing. I used to play soccer somewhere, I like to play soccer, but I must have that paper, work paper.

Me: Just to feel comfortable in your movement?

Immortel: Yeah, everywhere you go they need that paper, you know.

A report submitted to the High Court in Cape Town by the Department of Public Works looked at the viability of temporary camps, with at least 52 border crossings identified as potential sites. However, given the context that "South Africa doesn't have the resources to provide houses and food for our own citizens, let alone housing and feeding and schooling for thousands of asylum seekers in remote rural areas" (ibid), the feasibility of such an approach is dire. This approach represents the extent to which the South African state has strayed away from the basic traditional concepts of the Convention, transforming the refugee protection regime entirely from one of legal protection to one that denies asylum seekers their rights by socially and spatially excluding them from access. Coupled with the nuanced promotion of "voluntary deportation" evidenced by long-term detention and a lack of access to rights, seclusion and deportation perpetuate the assumption that non-nationals are economic migrants and are therefore not entitled rights (Monson and Arian, 2011: 51). The notions of seclusion and deportation as a humanitarian response to migrants fail in the context of refugee rights.

3. 4 Mobility and…Freedoms?

Changes in the world over the past fifty years have fostered new uses of the concept of the sovereign nation-state, which has had profound implications towards refugee protection. Disjunctures between space, place, citizenship and nationhood have led to increasing territoriality as a rationale for state legitimacy and power (Appadurai, 2003: 341). Sovereignty is increasingly used to overrule international institutions - to consolidate power - leading to a generalized lack of political will to protect migrants and lagging moral commitment to the refugee protection framework. This is demonstrated through the implementation of bureaucratic boundaries that limit access to rights, perpetuating a state of "bare life" for people without state protection. Together these factors have hindered the capacity of civil society and other legal aid organizations to play their role in protecting persecuted and displaced people worldwide and to monitor refugee protection within state borders, leading to a situation of "self-integration" and "self-protection" in zones of migration such as Bellville's CBD.

One would think that in a time when war transcends borders, leaving it mark on the geographic region through physical and virtual networks, that this should expand the responsibility-to-protect to states who may respond by protecting refugees as a bold political statement, as a mark of their "soft" political power. It is ironic that we should have increasingly stateless people in a time of ever more states and territories, human in-hospitality in a world of economic conviviality, like frost in a time of sunshine. However, an ethnographic study of Bellville's central business district disproves many of these general trends of hostility towards migrants. While intimate relationships between international migrants and the South African state are characterized by experiences of institutional, legal and administrative barriers to rights, hostility is allegedly refuted in the context of Bellville. Bellville is overwhelmingly described by migrants as "safe". The central business district of Bellville is a place where economic conviviality, social networks and bonding and bridging social capital prove the resilience of migrants in the face of trends towards exclusion. As the next chapter will explore, there is most certainly sun in this time of sunshine in Bellville, as conviviality emerges in the interface of exclusion and inclusion.

4

Convivial Spaces, Social Places

This chapter explores the narrative experiences and the social dynamics of daily life in the Bellville central business district, a place of accommodation and hospitality for migrants despite exclusion elsewhere. I argue that the notion of "place" is critical to understanding the meaning of Bellville as embodying the outcomes of institutional, legal and administrative barriers. The place itself is representative of how international migrants "make a plan" when mobility meets strict boundaries for exclusion. Bellville, as a space of mobility, is a place shared by international and South African migrants as well as "locals" and people passing through. While discourses of localism are often employed in the context of diversity in Bellville, this does not always reinforce difference. Instead, mutual need necessitates the building of relationships for both social and economic purposes, leading to interdependency and social cohesion in many circumstances. While the Bellville CBD does offer places of disinterest – where conviviality is not upheld, and where social tension, crime, and hostility do manifest – I argue that conviviality emerges in Bellville out of the negotiating of shared physical space. Manifested through economic interdependency, social capital and local governance mechanisms, conviviality emerges in the Bellville CBD to signify its role as a supportive and inclusive "place-based" society for migrants in Cape Town. Despite the continued narrative of "us" and "them" in Bellville, such national and social differencing rests on a foundation of conviviality through interdependent structures that are often crafted out of mutual interest. This chapter aims to identify the emergence of and opportunities for understanding conviviality, accommodation and tolerance within sites of diversity such as the Bellville CBD (SANPAD, 2011).

4. 1 Localizing Bellville

South Africa has experienced a retreat into localism that is represented by increasingly fragmented physical and social spaces of the urban landscape. Cape Town in particular, continues to endure urban separation and social segregation, characterized by a divisioning of society based on identity, what Arturo Escobar (2008) terms a "political ecology of difference." Despite a discourse of "inclusivity" and "democratic practice", the city continues to suffer from the effects of the Apartheid past, which manifest thorough spatial distancing and social non-interaction amongst groups (Morgan et al, 2013). Further, the trends towards a discourse of cosmopolitanism are, quite surprisingly, often refuted by hardened ideas of who belongs where, with whom and under what conditions.

Ousted from the nation and excluded from accessing their rights to public institutions, migrants in Bellville have consolidated their own networks based on kinship, region of origin, or economic ties to maintain a certain degree of relative autonomy. Transnational networks have assisted international migrants in Bellville to become successful entrepreneurs and businesspeople in the informal economy. Determined to succeed despite hardship, migrants in Bellville rely on innovation, business skills and mechanisms of group hospitality in order to enhance prospects for success. Information and communications technologies (ICTs) have also assisted migrants in maintaining social, family and business networks which play an integral role in establishing livelihood and income generating opportunities when in a new environment. For example, it is often a challenge for non-national migrants, and migrants with refugee status in particular, to open bank accounts (in those banks that *do* allow refugees access) due to the administrative time-lags involved in securing necessary documentation. The process requires the bank to confirm the immigration status of the applicant with the Department of Home Affairs, a timely and virtually untenable process due to management information systems within the Department of Home Affairs. The inaccessibility of a personal bank account is but one example of how urban predicaments exclude migrants from formal employment channels.

As a result of this administrative struggle as well as a general distrust in the formal banking system, Somalis in South Africa often carry out financial transactions in shops, businesses and warehouses owned by a trusted brotherhood through a system of *Hawala*. It is a remittance system that enables the transfer of money amongst family and business networks globally – Somalis in South Africa intimately engage with the diaspora around the world through this system. It takes a few phone calls and one to two days for the money to be transferred internationally. It is commission based for those involved but requires no paper work, and is based entirely on trust, efficiency and the strategic location of remittance networks. *Hawala* represents an example of how the mobile phone revolution and the rise of digital networking have contributed significantly to the growing prominence of network-based economies and informal trade in urban places. Network-based systems enable migrants to maintain critical support networks transnationally and to maintain financial security. As Jayaram notes, networks function as resource pools and insurance mechanisms in the urban world that is filled with risks and uncertainties (Jayaram, 2009).

Transnational networks are critically supported by information and communications technology (ICTs). Jayaram proposes that the value of social networks may be determined by access to bandwidth, and categories such as "bandwidth advantaged and disadvantaged" and "digital hermits" may be useful to describing the connectivity of communities (Jayaram, 2009). Bellville may be described as "bandwidth advantaged" – there are several internet cafes and international call centres that offer low priced phone calls made via hand-held phones over internet lines. It was noted by Abdikadir that, "In 2009, Somalia was one of the leading internet users globally, we mostly use social networks." One international call centre owner established his business two years ago. He explained, "People in Bellville call all over the world, mostly Kenya, Somalia, Europe and America. We provide an important service". Bellville is an internationally connected locality, transnational in every way through its diaspora populations that are increasingly representative of emerging cosmopolitanisms. This was evident to me in my first observations of Bellville when I noticed that Al Jazeera is a popular news channel played in several public restaurants. As Abdul, a Somali journalist who worked for Somali National Television and who now lives in Bellville, explained to me, "With Al Jazeera you can learn about Somali and Kenyan news. Many Somalis live in Kenya, you see, and we want to know what is going on." He remarked further, "In townships a lot of people watch local stations which are full of television dramas. We are looking for the international news." Migrants in Bellville are globally-minded, perhaps because their lives are influenced by the outcomes of geopolitics in many ways. Bellville represents the idea that the "local is not just the other of the global" but rather that the local and the global interact to produce spaces that are representative of global flows (Parthasarathy, 2009; Piot, 1999).

Figure 6: International Call Centre in Bellville

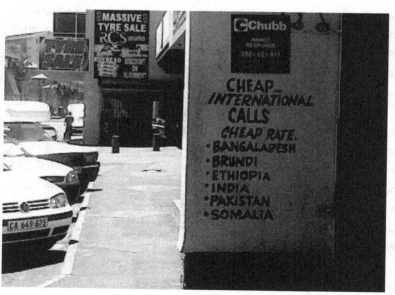

4. 2 Theorizing, Mapping and Historicizing Bellville

Theorizing Space and Place

It is essential to ask -- What is the meaning of space? What is the nature of place-making in Bellville's central business district? The social, political and economic factors as well as the history of the place are critical factors in an analysis of the active role people play in creating a social space. The production of space is a collective project shaped by interests of different classes, perspectives, histories, the grassroots and other contending forces. "Space is produced and reproduced through human intentions, even if unanticipated consequences also develop, and even as space constrains and influences those producing it" (Molotch, 1993: 887). Through Henri Lefebvre, the theorizing of nation-space is hardly imaginable without analysis of the work of architecture, particularly in an urban space. In order to address Lefebvre, I draw upon Appadurai's concepts of urban space and architecture. He notes:

"The city is inextricably linked with the visual order of modernity, and with its ideas of movement, point of view, memory and sociality. The modern city may be regarded as a constant negotiation between points of view and forms of experience which share with the visual order the sense of multiplicities of perspective, different orders of transparency and pluralities of depth which are affected by the moving purposes of the viewer. Architecture, whose primary future is to imagine something where there was previously something else, is the primary professional custodian of the visual archive of urban possibilities" (Appadurai, 2009: 9).

Space, and the architecture that takes a formative stance in space, play a critical role in the production of shared knowledge, of culture, and of habitus in communal, political, and convivially contested spaces (Lefebvre, 1974). The built environment may provide a sense of order to the flexibility and adaptability of space (Frank and

51

Stevens: 2007). This section looks at the history of place as recalled from outside and from within and at the aesthetics and structures that shape Bellville's commercial business district. It asks how these structures serve to situate the social life of space to conceptualize the individual experiences and embodiment of habitus that emerge in such a place.

Mapping Conviviality, Historicizing Place

The geographic area of the research site includes three parallel streets that intersect at the meeting of their ends in the area that comprises the Bellville train station, taxi rank and bus station. It was necessary to identify the parameters of the field site, as the area is a large urban space with several main roads and a plethora of smaller intersecting streets. In order to maintain a detailed perspective of the community I intended to study, I decided to focus on a particular area that I observed as integral to Bellville as a transitory space (with people transiting in, out and through), as a commercial business district and as an urban public and social meeting space for a diversity of people.

Durban Road, central to the study, is prominently located off of Voortrekker Road. It has a number of large commercial stores closer to the Voortrekker Road, such as First National Bank and Bed City, as well as migrant-owned establishments such as the Somali restaurant Dur Dur. As the road extends closer to the train station, the shops are increasingly owned by non-national migrants, particularly Somalis, though many of these shops employ South African shopkeepers who work there daily. Merchandise for the most part include: female and male clothing (which make up a majority of shops), groceries, home-ware and electronics. The main buildings that house migrant-owned businesses are large plazas, including the main Eastern and Western Plaza, which stand facing each other on either side of the street adjacent to Bellstat Junction, Wonderful Plaza, Continental Plaza, Okavango Plaza, Medical Plaza, Oriental Plaza and Welcome Plaza. Surrounding the train station is a popular shopping mall known as Bellstar Centre. Inside a majority of the plazas one finds a labyrinth of shops, escalators, winding corners and mannequins with brightly coloured pants. While inside most plazas, the time of day is completely unknown, the twilight of eternal time is projected with the florescent lighting that produces a glare across our paths and interactions. There are no, or perhaps just few, windows. Oftentimes, electronic house and techno music can be heard in contrast to the Somali music which plays in the shops facing the street on the outside. One can only imagine that with the lights off, the surreal Welcome Plaza may seem like an urban club. Moms and daughters and families with small children often frequent the area, particularly on the weekend.

Figure 7: Fashion Pants

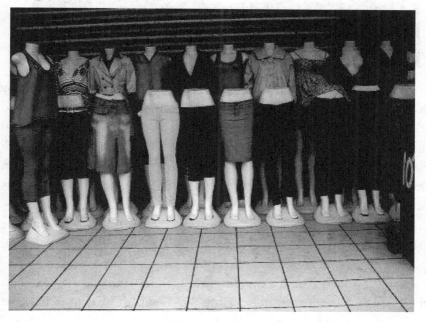

Figure 8: Women's Clothing Store

Durban Road's outdoor public space is mainly frequented by shopkeepers and shop-owners of all nationalities, customers and people hanging out outside of shops. Lots of deal-making and business is conducted right there on the street. Groups of Somali men make up a majority of people frequenting public space on Durban Road, perhaps due to its proximity to the mosque that is located next to the Western Plaza. Men hang out in large groups chatting or drinking coffee at the various coffee shops that line the streets and the top floors of plazas. The separation of people and space is hard to make in Bellville, as the streets are the heart of living – a critical space where everyday life unfolds (Jinnah, 2012a). This trend of congregation enables sharing of news and forms a sense of public community as people talk about subjects such as "living history, their place in it, their contribution to it from exile" (Farah, 2000: 86). There are also often groups of men loading armfuls of merchandise into a *bakkie*. Bellville is a warehousing site where stock is collected to supply migrant-owned shops, such as *spaza* shops, throughout the districts surrounding Cape Town. In some cases the stock may be so large that groups of men manoeuvre it into or on top of a *baakie*, others stop to watch or to help. Bellville is clearly a place of entrepreneurial spirit and of active business. It is a place where networking takes place between those who are personally included in the inner circle as an "insider". It is where groups of "insiders" may still relate to each other as "intimate strangers" – sharing close and overlapping spaces, but paradoxically, remaining relative strangers (Nyamnjoh, 2010). This negotiated interpersonal relationship forms the basis of conviviality.

Figure 9: Western Plaza

The plaza buildings on Durban Road are owned by Portuguese-South Africans who rented the space initially to Senegalese migrants before ownership shifted to (majority) Somalis around 1994. There is a high level of competition that takes place in order to secure ownership of a shop in a plaza. Somalis who initially migrated to South Africa in the early 1990s have either continued to maintain ownership over the years or have maintained partial ownership while allowing for newcomers from Somalia to "incubate" by working for their businesses in order to maintain financial standing before becoming self-sufficient to invest in their own businesses. Abdikadir explained, "There were maybe four Somalis, each with a 25% share, or then perhaps two would break away and open a new shop, then the original shop would be 50-50 ownership, but there was investment from the others. There was always a sense of trust, so it worked." It is a perpetual cycle that allows incoming migrants the security of livelihood and financial solvency in Bellville.

The main plaza buildings, such as Eastern Plaza, used to be huge warehouses in the past and were sub-divided in order to increase per-capita rental value. It was noted that Somali migrants are able to buy into these rental spaces because of their large pools of community funds. In funding their new businesses, many Somali entrepreneurs rely on their tradition of *biil,* which is interest-free money that Somalis pay to family and friends in need. *Biil* is also to pay for health care, rent, food or other needs for those who are unemployed or simply in need of help, particularly as newcomers (Huisman, Hough, Langellier, Toner, 2011: 186). It was described as "the same thing as family bills, like those that are paid monthly." As one of my contacts from Bellville, Omar, said during an interview, "When newcomers arrive, it is expected that the Somali community will help them, or that help will be provided. For Somalis, home is open. South Africans are more protective of their own business; disinterested and disengaged in others because of the Apartheid." Omar further explained that there is a group of decision makers selected in the Somali community, but they are not called "leaders" per say. These decision makers decide what contribution the community can provide to new or incoming Somalis from *biil* funds. This is an example of a support network that encourages the idea of "accommodating to be accommodated", a theme that is recurrent in my research and fieldwork. Somali decision makers in Bellville represent the "tendency towards dispersal and of managing tasks through long-distance networks" (Huisman et al, 2011: 26). This situation demonstrates the resilience of social capital amongst migrants.

According to several informants, developments in Bellville as a commercial hub of Cape Town have only taken place in the past eight years. "There has been a lot of architectural development – a lot more shops have opened recently." As a man from Pakistan with an electronics shop noted, "Before it was a mostly Afrikaans area, and there used to be a lot of *skollies* and crime." According to most respondents, "Foreigners bought into the area many years ago, and have since established a network of business owners and associations. Bellville is typically a first point of entry for newcomers to Cape Town and South Africa." The (South African) manager of one of the shopping centres noted of the area, "Immigrants are crucial to teach South Africans how to do business. The shop owners in Bellville are educated, hardworking, 'know how to work the book', and are "uplifting our people who are lazy." A Bangladeshi shop owner contributed to the conversation, noting "We are competing in a global market, you know? Bangladeshis migrate because of overpopulation at home – there is not enough business. We have money to invest and go on trips to see where we would like to immigrate to, we look for networks. The Somalis on the other hand, flee Al Shabbab and political persecution – they have no plan to leave." Insecurity, death in the family and even terrorism were overwhelmingly described as reasons for fleeing Somalia. However, the uniting factor between diverse communities of diaspora groups in Bellville is that, "it is just too dangerous (in townships) because people get jealous when we (foreigners) have anything going for us." Residents and shop owners claimed that Bellville is a good, safe environment to live in, as people share a common understanding of space. There is also a common understanding of what it takes to migrate and begin anew, of being nostalgic for "home" and of creating a new life in the context of hostility and perceived "outsiderness" by a suspicious public on the retreat into localism.

Figure 10: Hanging out in Bellville

Enhancing Conviviality through Public Support Structures

Prior to the migration of non-nationals and local traders to the area, the Bellville CBD was a primarily Afrikaans speaking community. The area that is now a thriving central business district previously accommodated a population characterized by low levels of employment, high illiteracy and crime. A senior librarian at the Bellville library, who used to coordinate an adult literacy programme, noted that, "Before 2009, the number of refugees in Bellville South was relatively low, and most of the refugees were literate and educated. We catered for many illiterate adults in the area who had no or very basic education." A Somali shop owner who has been in South Africa for eleven years described the changes, "Bellville has developed a lot in past years – there didn't used to be shops and there was more crime. Bellville is now safe but townships are not." He continued to compare the relative safety of Bellville today with insecurity faced by non-nationals in township life. "You may have six guys come up to you all with guns (in the townships); you can't sleep with that happening. You have to make friends with local blacks for security, you know, and then they watch out for you."

In addition to a thriving entrepreneurial and business community that has formed in Bellville's central business district around the train station, several commercial development and information technology projects are currently taking place in Bellville that may shift perceptions about the locality. A community centre was formed that can be accessed online via www. bellville-south. co. za, which is a physical and virtual portal to connect and communicate amongst Bellville's 30,000 residents. The Bellville-South Internet Project (BSIP), conceived of and implemented by a digital guru originally from Bellville as a social initiative, runs in association with the community portal. BSIP is not implemented in the commercial business district because "they have their own systems there", but residents are able to access services in residential areas. BSIP does not plan to venture into the CBD, as it would likely cause locally owned internet shops to go out of business. The goals of BSIP in the greater Bellville are to provide wireless internet connections to cover the geographic area of Bellville, to provide all residents with an email address under a common domain (e. g. Smith@bellville-south. co. za), and critically, to "put Bellville South on the world map. " The project aims to connect schools to high-speed internet and to establish internet cafes with computer literacy courses in order to build a computer and web-literate community. This initiative serves to increase communication and unification in diversity; a virtual manifestation of conviviality, linking ICTs to daily life.

Bellville also seeks to benefit from the extension of the city of Cape Town's "Urban Development Zone." This will involve public-private partnerships to improve public safety, cleaning of public space, public infrastructure and general regeneration of the area in order to attract investment, and thus job opportunities, into the area. These initiatives speak to Appadurai's (2006) notion of the "production of locality", with locality implying a "primarily relational and contextual, a phenomenological aspect of social life" to which public cleanliness, infrastructure and safety contribute (Amit, 2002: 3). This project comes at an opportune time, as many of the car patrollers voiced concerns about their own capacities in maintaining security in the area as well as the cleanliness of the streets. Such discourses of frustration have created concerns that are steeped in a discourse of "us" and "them". For instance, two female car patrollers emphasized how difficult it is to work in Bellville because "foreigners are rude and it is dirty in Bellville." One woman elaborated, "Sometimes we talk, laugh, and other times it is very hard to work here because the Somalis especially do not want to pay for parking. They park the whole day and then they drive off yelling and do not pay. " In the case of Bellville, the female car patrollers express frustrations due to their positions and responsibilities within the locality. This implies that the meaning people attribute to place and their membership in it has implications on intricate structures of relationships and modes of belonging (Cohen, 1985). As Cohen notes, "People construct community symbolically, making it a resource and repository meaning" (Cohen, 1985: 118). Drawing on Appadurai's vision of community as a "structure of feeling" (1996: 119), the impression of community in Bellville may be detached from actual social relations. In this sense, conviviality in Bellville is dependent on a "community of sentiment", in which individuals' personal relationships with place are dependent upon personal sentiments of society.

4. 3 Economic Conviviality in Bellville

National groups, including diaspora communities, immigrants and South Africans tend to associate socially in Bellville with people of their same nationality, particularly for business purposes. Often, this is the result of different business ethics and cultural rituals. As Anderson describes, "People tend to become integrated into webs of relationships through which they are able to function as individuals and as groups with a minimum of friction" (Anderson, 1960: 36). For instance, it was noted that Somalis and Tanzanians tend to not do business together because of different religious customs. Somalis follow daily prayer rituals and religious duties, and as Charles from Tanzania said, "Maybe if that Somali wants to close the shop for some time in the mid-day to do prayers, I am not ok with that and I cannot be expected to always be there to manage the situation."

60

Religion does, therefore, contribute to a discourse of difference. He elaborated further on why national groups tend to gravitate towards each other, "Outside of our home country, it is hard to build a community. It is hard to find consensus because we have different beliefs and represent different stakes for our people. For instance, if I arrange a meeting, perhaps it is agreed upon between everyone, but then only one person shows up. People have no time to waste on others in Bellville, time is money." He further noted that,

"Tanzanians tend to stick together, as all national groups in Bellville do. But it is also a common language that binds. For instance, in Kenya and East Africa they are speaking Swahili, just like we Tanzanians are speaking Swahili, so that binds us together here in South Africa. Like, if you go to somewhere else where they speak a foreign language and you meet non-South Africans speaking English, you will probably say like, hey I can speak to you in my language!"

However, Charles does collaborate with a South African woman from the Eastern Cape to sell goods at his vendor stall near the taxi rank. He explained that he wanted a woman to run his shop. Since there are not many Tanzanian women in Bellville (or perhaps in Cape Town), he hired a South African/Xhosa woman to sell his products which include belts, cell phone covers, hats and a myriad of other products. This tends to be common practice amongst non-national shop owners, who hire local shopkeepers in order to venture into new businesses themselves.

Figure 11: Vendor Stall on Charl Malan Street

Charles purchases his products from the Somali wholesale shops, which run off of vast networks mediated by Somalis worldwide; supply chains are controlled, from purchasing the goods, to arranging transport and clearing customs. It therefore became apparent that business interests *do* cross-sect national communities when in operation, though perhaps not theoretically. This is reflective of what Kay, a transnational migrant born in Tanzania and raised in the DRC, noted in a focus group discussion, "Everyone has their culture, but we live like family. We are scattered in views but we remain close and work together. Culture is there but we must not confuse culture with lifestyle." Business operations compel conviviality in Bellville, as they provide the ground for interactions, relationships and communality of interests. Groups work together not based on trust, but on necessity. As a Somali shopkeeper explained,

> "If you work together - you buy from him, he buys from you, you buy from the wholesale - these are all commercial relationships. It is a cash economy, so no trust is required.

Everything is traded upfront. It is in business partnership relations where trust is needed."

Commercial trading in Bellville is based on a mutuality of economic interest, and conviviality emerges due to the nature of accommodating to be accommodated. Conviviality is upheld out of economic necessity and is maintained by a melange of interdependent business interests.

4. 4 Emerging Cosmopolitanisms

Burdened by exclusive barriers to citizenship and difficulties in accessing protection and assistance in South Africa, highly mobile individuals self-integrate into society through business networks. Their livelihood activities – which are often formed through social networks – contribute to urban and grassroots economic development by generating income for local populations. Migrant-owned businesses often offer work opportunities to South Africans in surrounding areas, providing employment for labourers and to women in particular, who often face barriers to entering the workforce. Bellville's migrant networks and informal economy thus highlight the significance of migrant and refugee entrepreneurs and business owners to South African job seekers. Their story is one of conviviality – of mutual benefits arising from innovatively sidestepping away from tensions broiled in rhetoric of the "outsider". Bellville represents a newly formed "insider" group – one that rests at ease with "other" insiders and shifts the dynamics of "insiders" and "outsiders" to develop new meanings.

Figure 12: Kruskal Avenue on a Quiet Day

Vignette 2

Bellville's migrant networks and informal economy highlight the significance of migrant and refugee entrepreneurs and business owners to South African job seekers

Siphois from the Eastern Cape Province and came to Cape Town three years ago. He didn't know Bellville very well but came to the area to look for a job. He noted that, "You can get jobs in Bellville; there are lots of Somali shops. " The best thing about Bellville is that "there is too much business; there is nothing in the townships. " Bellville is known as a place of employment for both migrants and locals. Sipho used to work at Debonairs, a chain of pizza restaurants, but "the pay was too low. " This implies that Bellville's salaries are competitive.

Contrary to xenophobic trends in the general public that stigmatize foreigners, many South Africans and migrants of Bellville believe that migrant-owned businesses contribute significantly to the development of local economies. Several Somali shopkeepers in Bellville, for example, speak more than one South African language, which has perhaps helped to foster a dynamic of conviviality. Conviviality in urban spaces is thus enhanced by the strategic maintenance of networks; the resilience of migrants to adapt to new cities by learning local languages and by building a market within the informal economy. Conviviality is also enhanced by the appeal of Bellville to local consumers, who are drawn to low comparative prices and the job opportunities that arise for low skilled local workers. It is important to note that despite trends towards conviviality in Bellville, the same trends do not prevail in other communities of diversity. As a Somali shopkeeper and local leader noted, "There is a lot of xenophobia, but it is especially directed towards Somalis because we are developing this country. We are changing things, creating our own futures. In this situation, there will always be opposition. The situation improved from 2008, but now it is going back to the worst."

4. 5 Intimate Strangers and the Politics of Inclusion in Bellville

Bellville may be seen as a conglomeration of groups of "insiders" and "intimate strangers" (Nyamnjoh, 2010). Unlike other urban locations and informal settlements in Cape Town where xenophobia and the parameters of community are often expressed in terms of "us" and "them", the concept of an "outsider" does not present itself in the same way. The occupation of a shared urban space and similarities of motives for journeying towards a life in the city evoke an intimacy driven by collective experiences amongst diverse groups. As Mike from Ghana noted, "People live in Bellville because rent is cheap and we have community there. There is lots of violence in the locations. Amongst foreigners, we stick together because we have a lot of common experiences." However, intimacy is subjugated by the politics of belonging, creating tensions that forever hold "strangers" an arm-and-a-half-length away. Urbanites are like porcupines, their quills spanning out to protect against even the most-warm hearted neighbours. (Nyamnjoh and Brudvig, 2013: 14) Defensive quills create a "protective" barrier, reasserting notions of "self" and distancing from the "other", which may result in social non-interference. As one Somali man in Bellville expressed, "Humanity, human rights brings us together, let us share what we share and respect non-interference. If we have interference, none of us have security, a home..." Such is the basis of conviviality in Bellville, as it is encouraged by recognition of the potential for destructive relations and a preference of that which is mutually constructive.

Vignette 3

Their story is one of conviviality - of mutual benefits arising from innovatively sidestepping away from tensions broiled in rhetoric of the "outsider"

On the topic of community, one Ethiopian man noted, "There is no community; you see we just work with our own people here. Maybe in the future there will be more community. With community we could talk all together about business, social life in South Africa. I know a lot of locals; they like us because we are good to our customers and make them feel welcome. We know how to approach them but we may have different ideas about business, that's why we work with Ethiopians for business. "

He explained, "The problem with South Africa is the violence in the townships. The government must stand up for the refugee people. The refugee people, they don't make violence – they make cheaper prices to support South Africans. South Africans also learn from us how to open shops and make businesses. Many people are starting *lekker* business; they get our mind and our advice. Since being in Bellville, even I have learned to become more business minded. "

Despite the existence of a notion of the "other", this "other" is still considered an "insider". This analysis represents the degree of hospitality, of conviviality, that presents itself in Bellville amongst multi-ethnic communities. We may define "community" in Bellville not in terms of *Gemeinschaft*, in which "the emotive charge of community arises out of multiplex, long-standing interpersonal relationships of deep intimacy and familiarity" (Amit, 2002: 17), and not in terms of a convergence between culture, place, social relations and collective identity, but rather, in terms of Gupta and Ferguson's notion of community. They quote, "Community is never simply the recognition of cultural similarity or social contiguity but a categorical identity that is premised on various forms of exclusion and construction of otherness" (Gupta and Ferguson, 1997: 13). The nature of exclusion and "othering" offers opportunity, in a place of cosmopolitan identities, to define both collective and individual affiliations. With respect to space and place, this process of "othering" and of situating oneself in a space of "otherness" creates a place of meaning and sets Bellville apart from other places. Bellville, as a "community of belonging" is a "contested field of interaction and negotiation...fields of face-to-face social relationships and reflecting a great deal of individuality and active participation on the part of its members" (Amit, 2002: 127).

Different nationalities represented in Bellville, however, do seem to occupy business and livelihood niches in the products or services provided. Businesses start small, and expansion and entry into the broader market requires an effective mobilization of community resources. From my initial observations and conversations, the dynamics of insiders and outsiders appear to also occupy different, and somewhat defined, spaces within the Bellville train station and taxi rank vicinity. For instance, Somalis typically engage in wholesale trading, and their reach spans Bellville and extends to supply shops in nearby towns and in the townships. Ethiopian migrants own several restaurants and shops in the same common area as the Somalis. I met several Tanzanians who all own and run different barber shops, as a niche service. In a somewhat secluded area outside of the train station, I met several women from South Africa, migrants from the Eastern Cape, who claimed that their income from sales at their vendor stalls had suffered because of the space they are allocated "near Paint City", which is towards the back of the taxi rank and out of sight from the general public corridors. Claiming a space to engage in informal trade at the station is a struggle, as vendors pay rental costs and those who don't face eviction from "law enforcement". I asked Margaret from the Eastern Cape more about this. "Foreigners, this place is for them", she said. Indeed, non-nationals have large commercial interests and investments in Bellville, as well as leverage from support by their communities to expand. A food stand at the taxi rank that is run by a South African woman is soon to be run by Somali owners because they offered to pay higher rental fees for the business. Such situations have caused South African *spaza* shop owners to express resentment towards foreign micro-entrepreneurs in the market. Studies indicate that grievances are rooted in a "price-discounting war", in which the success of foreign-run shops has significantly curtailed the profitability of locally run shops due to the use of price discounting and strategic positioning of the shops (Charman and Piper, 2011: 3). The tension exists because of fundamentally different business practices. On the one hand, South African *spaza* shops maintain prices at levels which permit all shopkeepers equal opportunity; whereas foreign owned *spaza* shops substantially discount prices to attract customers. Charman and Piper refer to these two strategies as "survivalist" versus "opportunity driven" (2011: 4).

I noticed several different reactions to this type of economic competition, which represent a variety of perceptions that are critical to understanding the extent to which conviviality emerges in Bellville. A Somali shopkeeper explained,

"Some South Africans might ask, 'where did you get money?' when they should be asking, 'how did you start a business?' Somalis are natural entrepreneurs. When South Africans are in opposition, they lose out. It's like the saying goes, 'if you can't beat us, then join us'. This would be a better option. "

Several South African residents noted that the presence of foreign traders in Bellville is uplifting because of higher standards of business practice. The other side to the coin is the perception of intrusion. "It's like they are taking over Bellville." One South African man noted further, "They charge very low prices and take over the market. But locals, we South Africans, go there because at the end of the day, everyone is desperate for money and will go for the best deal." While many residents and mobile customers appreciate the lower prices, local shopkeepers become resentful because they are unable to match lower prices. This has led to a generalized feeling of distrust amongst South African *spaza* shop owners. A South African man in Bellville stated, "Other shop owners, South Africans, have to shut down. It is the low skilled local Africans that suffer." He elaborated that, "In South Africa, we have the capitalists, the businessmen, the middle class and the unskilled people – and they are hurt the most by this. This kind of competition hasn't gone to the top yet." Lefebvre might issue warning in response to this. He notes, "When relations of power overcome relations of alliance, when rhythms of 'the other' make rhythms of 'the self' impossible, then total crisis breaks out, with the deregulation of all compromises arrhythmia, the implosion-explosion of the town and the country" (Lefebvre, 2004: 99). Fervent competition arises out of inclusion or exclusion from systems of power, leading to the perception of economic threat. These perceptions are reminiscent of the propensity for xenophobia across South Africa.

4. 6 Arising Insecurities and Places of Disinterest

My analysis on space and place in Bellville has led me to consider that conviviality is maintained by individuals' carefully routinized spatial meanderings. One does not have to walk far to exit the convivial boundaries of Bellville's multicultural and diverse neighbourhoods. Conviviality exists at a neutral borderline that is fluid and occasionally erupts in threats, outrage and even violence. I was in a Somali-owned clothing store when two men entered the scene yelling, a provocative tone in their voices. They were asking in half Xhosa and half English, "Does this Somali shop have pillow cases. Pillllllooowwww cassesss. Do you know what that means Somali?" They were harassing the shop based on its foreign ownership, for there were clearly no pillow cases in a shop of women's clothing. In this instance, the shopkeeper was composed, and responded respectfully, "I'm sorry I don't speak Xhosa.... we don't have pillow cases, there are pillow cases in the shop down the street." The two hooligans left, muttering and puttering in their foolishness. The shopkeeper apologized to me and other shoppers, "They are drunk, this happens often".

In analysing emerging insecurities within the Bellville central business district, it is necessary to dwell on the taxi rank as a critical place where conviviality is contested. This particular area is analysed as a "heterotopic space" (Foucault, 2007). This became clear to me during mapping exercises, as the people I was with (who are non-nationals) were hesitant to cross a certain pathway into the taxi rank area, though they were always convivial in making sure that I would be safe on my own. One man explained, "Taxis are gangs. They cause a lot of violence in this area, even in the day. You might know someone for two years and then they shoot you. There is no trust in this community. " In his drawn map, Charles provided details of the inner cross streets of the area, though the taxi rank area is a big empty space in the corner, which signified to me his spatial boundaries.

In order to explore this social dynamic of space, I interviewed a taxi driver who transits in and out of Bellville several times a day. My informant, Zamani, explained that internal taxi violence often results in public fights. Some taxi operators own two taxis and others own twelve. "So the ones with fewer taxis get less business, the others are monopolizing the business. Those of us with only few taxis have to wait like four hours for a full load. And then we overload by like six people to make ends meet. So there is internal conflict and the guys are taking each other out." In his opinion, "The taxi rank is the safest place of Bellville – if anyone steals from you then others will see and they will protect you." Furthermore, there is an informal office at the taxi rank in Bellville where "if any taxi driver upsets a customer, the customer can report it to this office and the driver will get the shit beaten out of him." The taxi industry represents a site of relatively more hostility and uncertainty in particular for non-nationals, but also for migrants from other parts of South Africa, as described in Vignette 4 below. This contrasts with other areas in Bellville that have become sites of ownership and empowerment for a diverse community of nationals and non-nationals. The functionality of the taxi industry as a public service and as a central landmark in Bellville is dependent upon a fine line of conviviality. As a multitude of travellers pass in, out and through, each day the taxi stand becomes a place of intense negotiation and interaction, sometimes good and sometimes bad.

Vignette 4

The taxi industry represents a site of relatively more hostility and uncertainty in particular for non-nationals

Patrick works on Durban Road as car patroller. He described the taxi rank as "very dangerous" - there was emphasis and emotion in his face as he spoke about the insecurity. "It's bad over there by the train station, there are criminals and *skollies*...you see them there hanging out. " He is from the Eastern Cape and lived in Gauteng for some time. He elaborated that, "The problem in Cape Town is that there are so many *skollies*, there is lots of stealing and crime at the taxis. Where I stayed just outside of Joburg, this just didn't happen. "

4. 7 The Influence of "Community" on Conviviality

Experiences of migration and urban mobility are often characterized by personal transitions, including de-socialization and re-socialization of the self. De-socialization may lead individuals to invest in preserving their identities, fervently recreating familiar lifestyles by guarding ethnic and religious identity, often in isolation from local society. In parallel processes of re-socialization, individuals assimilate to local customs and develop emerging and fluid multicultural identities (Huisman et al, 2011: 83). The role of community to individuals during periods of cultural transitions is of great significance, as it offers the promise of belonging. Feeling a sense of belonging is important not only for safety and comfort, but in terms of people's interrelatedness and willingness to provide hospitality and generosity. A community's well-being, the quality of relationships and cohesion that exists, depends on social capital, referring to social networks based on reciprocity and mutual trust (Putnam, 1993). Networks of support, which are often found in urban diaspora enclaves such as Bellville, represent a form of social capital that creates norms towards greater mutuality. Channels of social capital are critical to maintaining conviviality in Bellville, as they create a site for belonging for a diversity of people. A sentiment of belonging may be described as, "To be welcome, even if we are strangers. As if we came to the right place and are affirmed for that choice" (Block, 2009: 3). Conviviality is thus upheld by a sense of community affirmation through network-based relationships.

Figure 13: Road Leading to the Taxi Rank

On the contrary, for many South Africans, Bellville is a place of territorial stigma, described as simply, "A place that we come through." One man noted that, "Bellville is not a 'community'...maybe it is for the Somalians, but for us, it is just a place we pass through...maybe for work or shopping." Further, it was stated that, "Bellville is a transit point for taxis - that is why there are so many different people. They transit from locations, just like Cape Town is also a transit point." Addressing Bellville as a "community" to local South Africans often instigated a discourse of "us" and "them", as well as a denial of the existence of community in Bellville. It was attributed that non-nationals often reside in Bellville because "*they* (foreigners) don't like the townships because *they* are scared of us." However, a sense of community does emerge amongst a diverse migrant and non-migrant population in Bellville. Community and conviviality emerge in Bellville due to the dynamics of social capital and forms of local governance that encourage notions of inclusion and belonging. The social fabric of community in Bellville is shaped by a shift in discourse away from social boundaries. Conviviality emerges in the frequent interplay between dynamics of group-autonomy on the one hand and an interdependent communalism of groups on the other hand. It is also deeply rooted to the particular dynamics of space, place and community in Bellville.

Conviviality rests on a fine line of tolerance and respect for each other's movement and use of public space, offering the possibility of restoring trust in neighbours, faith in leaders and a discourse of hospitality that is upheld by cosmopolitan multiculturalism. This reflects a degree of "social cohesion". According to the African Centre for Migration and Society,

> "A cohesive community is not necessarily one in which everyone likes, trusts or agrees with everyone else. Instead, distrust, tension and conflict will always exist between various in-groups and out-groups. Therefore, rather than seeing social cohesion as a – somewhat unrealistic – state in which conflict and dissent are eradicated, we consider social cohesion – at its most fundamental level – to be about the way in which a community of diverse sub-groups deal with (inevitable) social tensions and conflicts" (Monson et al, 2012: 19).

Given this analysis, it is important to consider what mechanisms may be used to further enhance trends towards social cohesion in Bellville in the context of general inclinations towards localism, group preservation and xenophobia. Building viable social cohesion involves supporting the organic ways in which social capital is cultivated in Bellville. To achieve this, civil society in Bellville requires structured methods for communicating new visions for shared space – so that "street-friendly people" may transform Bellville into a place of "people-friendly streets" (Cape Times, 2013). Building social cohesion requires supporting individuals who have the skills and capacity to mobilize civic discourse through community participation and engagement. Supporting diversity and the implementation of democracy in this regard requires an understanding of the dynamics of social capital and local governance at the micro-level.

Social Capital and Local Governance amongst Somali Migrants in Bellville

Somali migrants comprise a majority population in Bellville's central business district and have a prominent presence in the area. The Somali Association of South Africa estimates that there are over 30,000 Somalis residing in South Africa. With at least 15,000 Somalis residing in Cape Town, it may be assumed that many Somali migrants in Cape Town reside or have resided in Bellville at some point in time. Many Somalis in Bellville are young, and it was explained to me that Somali youth in their twenties and thirties comprise a majority of migrants. They may realize that they have their whole futures ahead of them, and limited prospects for education, work and for a family in Somalia. "So they leave in an act of rebellion to change their lives for the better." As Abdikadir explained, "The new generation has more freedom, the world is opening doors." Migration is not a new phenomenon for Somalis. Bellville Somalis noted that mobility has always been a way of life, based on historically nomadic lifestyles in which movement takes place within dense kin and clan networks (Huisman et al, 2011: 26). This is expressed linguistically through the term *buufis*, which is used to express a longing to move – it may also refer to a sense of stress which results from an unsatisfied desire to travel (Jinnah, 2012a: 1). Furthermore, Somali forced migration is a result of civil war in Somalia that has persisted for decades. Civil war in Somalia is fuelled by "centuries-old injustices; decades-old political feuds; Siyad's tyrannical state, and its indifference to the ordinary people's genuine grievances; the nature of post-colonial set-ups" (Farah, 2000: 45). Nuruddin Farah elaborates further on the circumstances of war in Somalia. He writes, "High principles have been pushed aside and…in their place, people have begun putting their faith in the pornography of a warlord's rhetoric, holding forth and reciting chapters and verses of clan mythography. Civil wars do not wait for reasons. They erupt, they happen" (ibid). A lack of state presence in Somalia over past decades has destabilized much of the country and citizenry, leading to increased migration flows as a survival response.

Somalis have successfully adapted centuries-old migration strategies into the dynamics of their modern mobility. These strategies are necessary for economic survival, and they have become translated into business and governance practices. Dispersed into a diaspora spanning the world, Somalis maintain successful regional trade networks, often based upon kinship relations that facilitate access to consumer goods and low prices. A Somali woman that I spoke to in Bellville stated, "Even if a Somali has no formal education, they are good at survival and this translates to business skills." Because of trends towards migration, Somalis have cultivated strong systems of hospitality that are embedded in family and clan ties. It was explained to me that once a Somali migrant arrives in a new place, it is common practice to find or call some other Somali contact within the locality either through referral or by going to a point of communal networking, such as Bellville. The first contact that is established is then responsible for referring the newcomer to someone of their same clan who will be responsible to provide assistance and hospitality. Cell phones play an important role in this networking process and a flurry of phone calls take place until the newcomer has a host. It was noted that the only downside to this is that, "Your phones are never going to be quiet because you will get calls at night at home about someone coming in" (Huisman et al, 2011: 43). Somali migrants are able to draw upon social conventions that cultivate networks through hospitality in order to build relations and ease into daily life in Bellville.

The clan system is used to identify relatives and to find support by tracing each other back generations through an orally recounted lineage. As Abdikadir explained, it is used for "finding out who is who." He explained further, "It is expected that any Somali can go to another and will be hosted for a week or so. But at the end of the day, you have to be a man and help yourself. Since there are so many Somalis now, you can usually find someone of your clan; otherwise you just go to any Somali." The importance of clan in Somali heritage creates a situation where individuals immediately experience a degree of belonging as they are welcomed by a member of their clan who is considered family. I sought to understand what the difference is between the main clan groups. How do these groups express difference or commonality in identity? It was explained to me in Bellville that,

> "Difference is not expressed in a straight forward way. In the West and in many societies, difference is expressed through politics. In Somalia, clan was often used to create enemies. When the dictator was removed, the opposition used clans to incite difference and to gain power. But differences are less prevalent in South Africa because we are out of our own context. There is no way of expressing difference or using it – maybe only in the heart."

As Nuruddin Farah writes, "The clan is seen as both the evil common denominator and an explicator of all actions, good and bad, as well as an indispensable form of social organization" (2000: 14). However, for the Somali community in Bellville, clan hospitality has led to increased "bonding social capital" (Putnam, 1993), a condition necessary for the group to develop confidence in its own abilities and dealings with other groups (Steenkamp, 2009: 444).

Bonding social capital, most evident through trust, is critical to business practices in Bellville, and is an integral part of public and social life. "It is trust that makes a Somali business succeed." It was explained that, "Those who are not trustworthy will have their name destroyed – they become street boys with no prospects for further employment. Trust drives everything. If someone has not been loyal, everyone will find out about it. You can lose a lot without trust." Somali business owners often conduct background checks before hiring new shopkeepers. A trustworthy partner is critical because, "In business you always need someone to watch the shop when the owner has to pray or use the toilet. Sometimes we get friends to watch over the shop, if they do a good job maybe they will be compensated R200 and good rapport is made." It was further explained that there is a system for "testing" someone that is suspected of stealing money from the shop. In this case the owner may leave the employee or partner in the shop alone for three months to prove his trust to the business. "He can't run away, because they would know his family, his tribesmen." In this trial period, one is able to redeem trust and self-pride. This represents the importance of reputation to belonging, as well as the significance of gossip as a form of social control that contributes to belonging (de Vries, 1995: 36). As Merry (1984) suggests, the impact of gossip is greatest when it has the potential of producing a community consensus that can be converted into collective actions against the individual, such as shaming, ridicule or expulsion. Further, the impact of scandals are greater in social settings where the members of the local system are more interdependent for economic aid, jobs, political protection and other social support (Merry, 1984: 296). Bonding social capital – maintained through trust, the preservation of identity and the desire to belong – is therefore critical in maintaining social and economic conviviality.

In addition to "bonding social capital", in which there exists deep trust and frequent interaction between individuals who identify with the group, Somalis in Bellville have also created various mechanisms for inclusion that emphasize "bridging social capital" (Putnam 2003). "Bridging social capital" refers to sufficient trust between the individuals belonging to different groups to facilitate cooperation (Steenkamp, 2009: 444). Mechanisms that facilitate inclusion and cooperation amongst groups include the Somali Association of South Africa, the Somali Sunni Mosque and informal governance mechanisms facilitated by appointed intermediaries. These civil society associations in Bellville collaborate to bridge formal relationships with other groups in order to have a platform for negotiation on common issues. They have facilitated a "radius of trust" amongst cooperating agents (ibid), thus contributing to conviviality through mechanisms of inclusion. The re-building of social networks may be considered as linked to shifting identities, particularly related to self-identification – as being, for example, Somali first and Muslim second, or aligned with Muslims from other countries. Frank and Stevens (2007) argue that public spaces such as the Bellville CBD encourage an exploration of identity.

Figure 14: A Mosque in Bellville

The Somali Association of South Africa (SASA) and the Somali Women's Organization play critical roles in leadership and advocacy for the Somali diaspora and migrants in general. One leader of the group became a formative member of SASA after being recognized as a leader by the community. He explained, "They look at how other people carry themselves." Leaders are often chosen based on their perceived wisdom, oratory skills and personal qualities that command respect and authority (Huisman et al, 2005: 84). At first he shied away from leadership. "In a foreign country, you cannot lead the way you want to lead ideally. There are some problems that you just cannot resolve for people. The challenges are many – for instance much of the community are non-citizens. I am also not a lawyer to be able to fight for rights. I am here to be a voice, to help anyone." Community leaders are often called upon to oversee conflicts and to negotiate outcomes with parties. A system of conflict resolution is reminiscent of fragmented political leadership in Somali, in which case pockets of social hierarchal structures were present to govern (Huismanet al,

2005: 84). It was explained that the conflicts are usually about business, such as if there is a suspected low turnover due to theft, but sometimes they are about other issues. A conflict can take up to several weeks to resolve. It involves a recruitment of chosen conflict mediators from the Somali diaspora spanning across South Africa to travel to the city or town where the conflict is taking place. In the process of negotiation, "You have to make them see eye to eye." It was explained that one learns how to do this only through experience, so oftentimes the elders of the community are called to assist. In a recent case, elders were invited from Johannesburg to Port Elizabeth to assist in negotiating a conflict. It is generally men who are involved in this system, but "women have their own system of elders who sort out conflicts." Public life is dependent upon community-based citizenship initiatives such as local governance mechanisms to foster community participation and engagement.

The Somali Women's Organization is led by a woman who has been in Cape Town for eleven years and identified the need to support Somali women in Cape Town. The leader seeks to create channels to communicate issues and concerns that have arisen, particularly relating to helping Somali women access health services and educational opportunities for children. She lamented, "There are pregnant women, women who have had a baby and now have psychological difficulty. Women may go to the hospital and some people have allegedly claimed to have been turned away if a nurse doesn't like foreigners. Then the woman goes home with her sick baby and waits for days perhaps." Furthermore, it has been alleged that, "Often schools say to foreigners, 'no, we are full' and they turn the mother and child away." These occurrences are by no means evidence of institutionalized discrimination, but are merely exceptional situations that Somalis and other migrants have experienced in the past. The leader of the organization assists in these situations by intervening to establish a clear system of communication on the issues. There are about sixty women who are currently involved in the activities of the Somali Women's Organization. Since many women also work in shops, it is difficult to schedule meetings, so the leader often passes by different shops where women are based to chat and "hear people's stories." The main problem that arises is that "many refugees don't know their rights." The experience of forced migration significantly alters the social environment within which women's rights are framed, including sexual and reproductive rights, leading to the likelihood that they are not claimed (Jinnah, 2012c). The organization is critical to encouraging autonomy for Somali women. In doing so, it further influences the negotiation of gendered identities within cultural and religious discourses (Jinnah, 2012c). Such channels of support engage Somali women to encourage self-development, assimilation and conviviality amongst men and women in Bellville.

These leadership structures have the potential to contribute to meeting the needs of Somali migrants in South Africa. Innovative use of the internet further represents democratic forms of engagement that encourage both "bonding" and "bridging" social capital. It was noted by a community leader that in 2009, Somalia was one of the leading internet users worldwide. He explained, "We mostly use social networks." Digital technology has supported emerging leaders and enhanced entrepreneurial traits, such as their ability to cope with risk and uncertainty, creativity in problem solving and collaborative efficiency in the use of community resources (Huisman et al, 2005: 96). Leaders emphasize bridging social capital, which is inclusive and outward-looking in order to build social networks outside of one's immediate "group". These contemporary leaders differ from traditional Somali leadership, which is structured within a council of elders (*guudiga*). While alternative forms of leadership do not replace traditional leadership structures, contemporary leaders do play a critical role in demonstrating the adaptability of Somali migrants in Bellville. Leaders are globally minded, professional and fully conversant in English (and other South African languages). Nuruddin Farah's description of a "generation (of Somalis) in their late twenties and early thirties, go-getting, ambition-driven men and women...prepared to clean up the political mess others had created" (Farah, 2000: 37) is perhaps fitting. Contemporary community leaders emphasize the importance of working within and outside of the direct community to establish trust and to strengthen relationships and networks. This approach to working within and outside the community aligns contemporary leaders with strategies (such as those regarding social capital suggested by Robert Putnam) that are essential for developing a strong civil society (Huisman et al, 2005: 94). The Bellville Education Centre is one example of the how the Somali Association of South Africa has initiated the formulation of relationships within the migrant community – including the non-English speaking community of Bellville, as well as with those who wish to improve their English language. They have also integrated horizontally with other NGOs in civil society that provide education services for refugees in Cape Town. While innovation emerges from informal structures, formal structures, such as the Bellville Education Centre, are significant to insuring sustainability and growth (Frank and Stevens: 2007).

4. 8 Dynamics of Gender in Bellville: Seeking a Woman's Perspective

Many of the women who I interacted with and interviewed in Bellville were South African traders and shopkeepers. They are often the "bread winners" of their families and come to Bellville because "it is a business place" and they face a lot of competition when selling in other parts of town. In one case, three women were selling scarves and kitchen cloths, *lappies*. They were mobile, without a table or shop, and surrounded me, seemingly identifying their new location for selling their products. I asked, "How did you decide where to sell?" One woman explained the informal rules of space and place for hawkers and traders, citing the difficulty experienced by (primarily) South African women who may have little financial backing and are unable to rent a formal space for trade in Bellville. She explained, "We are only supposed to sell there by Paint City (next to the taxi rank), but it is very quiet, so we come here and move around. But law enforcement is the problem." She explained that she has been selling goods in Bellville for twelve years. "In Bellville there is no work, but there is business." Bellville provides a critical market for otherwise unemployed mothers who depend upon the flexibility of space and place that they are able to capitalize on in the central business district of Bellville. They are mobile within the locality, undefined by spatial boundaries, but alert to the presence of police and other officials in space who are able to capitalize based on their power of authority. These mobile women lead us to consider that "different modes of occupying space imply different modalities of sociality and sociability" (Ross, 2010: 62). Their movements intersect the informal and formal dynamics of territory in Bellville. Their relationship to space, and people within space, is fluid and constantly negotiated based on notions of sociability and conviviality.

Somali Women in Bellville

Since a majority of Bellville's non-national community is of Somali heritage, I felt that it was imperative to endeavour to understand general perspectives of Somali women in Bellville. These perspectives are often of the private realm, and underlie the basis of conviviality in the public. Women's perspectives highlighted many dynamics of personal, home and family life that are often excluded in a male perspective. Stories from women in Bellville, as most stories from migrants, begin in the middle – the story is already underway and continues to unfold with time. Several of the young women with whom I spoke arrived in South Africa alone, and have since reconnected with distant relatives such as aunts and uncles, though close family members remain in places prominent to the Somali diaspora, such as Kenya and Minnesota in the United States. Families often become separated due to violence encountered and the perils of forced migration. As a result, many women work in shops and own stalls in the streets in Bellville to support themselves and family. One woman who came to Cape Town alone explained that she didn't have any options but to pay someone to smuggle her in a truck. She explained, "I paid a lot of money, so it was ok – but we didn't have passports so we had no other option." She travelled via Kenya, Tanzania and Zambia before entering South Africa.

Somali woman in Bellville are generally of the sentiment that, "Bellville is beautiful. I don't like Cape Town, but I love Bellville." Bellville provides a sense of security, particularly for Somali women who either do not speak proficient English or who are in South Africa on their own without a husband. A woman named Idman, dressed in black dress with a bright yellow hijab, was selling men's clothing in a shop. She is Somali and had ten children, but explained to me that three had died and the other seven are still in Somalia. She claimed to have come to South Africa "because of Al Shabbab". It was very unsafe for her in Somalia and her husband was killed. She demonstrated this by making a slit motion across her throat. Bellville provides opportunities for Idman to maintain a livelihood and to support her children. She has less to fear in her daily movements in Bellville, as it has become a place of familiarity due to the presence of, particularly Somali, migrant social and business communities. The vast presence of the police – who patrol the streets, pen and notepad in hand, alert to the arising insecurities that do emerge in Bellville – also provide a sense of physical security for Somali women. Somali women attribute their safety in Bellville to the widespread presence of the police, amongst other community development and social networking channels that provide relative freedom to pursue livelihoods, particularly for single or widowed women.

Somali men also believe that Bellville is a safer place for women, because "there is a lot of crime in the townships and it is not safe for women and children." This was a widespread opinion that emerged time and time again and without contradiction. It is important to note that, in general, men maintain responsibility over women in terms of protection and support (Jinnah, 2012c). In dating relations, singles may meet to chat about family and their desires in the future, many chat on their phones via Whatsapp, Facebook and sharing photos, but there is no intimacy allowed. Friends and love interests may not be of the same Somali clan or national heritage, and conviviality does emerge through friendship and relationships. In terms of marriage, a most important rite, it was explained to me that, "Women are red meat and men are like hyenas, to avoid the woman being eaten, she must get married!" A man may marry outside of Islam, but a woman cannot without giving up her religion, which is inherited paternally. This is based on the premise that a man marries a woman and can therefore choose who to marry, Muslim or not. However, Somali men and women both have the power to divorce, and it was explained to me by a woman that she could kick out her husband if she wished. It was highlighted that many Somali men marry outside of their culture and religion in South Africa. Such relations represent a most intimate form of conviviality. However, the situation is more problematic for Somali women, as these relationships are generally not supported by women's families. A local informant provided an example of a Somali woman and a Chinese man in South Africa who fell in love and wanted to get married. When the proposition was presented to the woman's family, her father refused. As a result, the family moved away to prevent any further communication between the couple. These factors of intimate life translate into a greater freedom of choice for Somali men in South Africa. However, living in a diaspora provides an opportunity to redefine and reinterpret nationality and cultural heritage (Jinnah, 2012c) for both men and women. As such, Somali women play a critical role in negotiating between various culturally relevant social environments to produce new social and economic norms for the diaspora community.

4. 9 Sociality and the Territory of Convivial Space

Social isolation of migrants in South Africa has propagated a discourse of difference, as migrants are approached as belonging to religious or cultural groups with more or less constant and clearly discernible features (Sunier, 1995: 60). As a result, migrants perceive themselves as different because society has internalized an apparent ideal of the nation-state. A discourse of difference has led to popular perceptions of migrants as perpetual "newcomers", as differences in culture and religion are identified as having been brought from countries of origin. Seen as never quite belonging even if they have lived most of their lives in a host-country, "migrants (or those with the wrong race, ethnicity of geography) feel more and more vulnerable to the growing popularity of the extreme right and of anti-immigration and racial or ethnic purity politics and the policies of various states" (Nyamnjoh,2006: 229). Fear, vulnerability and the imperative to maintain personal safety are the factors underlying the reclamation of space by migrants in Bellville's central business district.

Migrants in Cape Town, including refugees, are often rejected by local society, accused of compounding problems of joblessness and demand for scarce resources within the city. As a result of the combination of a refugee policy that promotes "integration" into local society and widespread institutionalized discrimination, migrants have managed nonetheless to forge multi-stranded social and economic relations that link together their countries of origin, countries of asylum, and countries where family and networks reside (Campbell, 2006: 125). As a result of relative independence, facilitated by strong social capital and networking, Bellville has become a commercial centre for migrants involved in the informal economy, selling consumer goods galore and offering a majority of services imaginable at the cheapest price in all of Cape Town. Bellville's CBD, which not long ago was a depressed area, is now the epicentre of a booming formal and informal economy. Immigrant entrepreneurs have reconstructed the built environment, transforming what was once an area of general disinterest into a thriving hub for informal trade that serves the best interests of local South Africans and migrants (Murray and Myers, 2006: 121). With the best prices in town, South African consumers and merchants are increasingly dependent upon the low cost goods and services provided largely by urban migrants.

Several different perspectives have emerged on why Bellville is a zone of migration – a destination for immigrants, migrants from within South Africa and commuters within Cape Town. These anecdotes demonstrate how meaning becomes attached to place. It is not the space of Bellville that necessarily draws people towards it, but it is the place – the meaning ascribed to that space by lived history, shared understandings and a de-territorialized sense of home. As Gupta and Ferguson write, "The irony of these times is that as actual places and localities become ever more blurred and indeterminate, ideas of culturally and ethnically distinct places become perhaps even more salient. It is here that it becomes most visible how imagined communities come to be attached to imagined places, as displaced peoples cluster around remembered or imagined homelands, places, or communities in a world that seems increasingly to deny such firm territorialized anchors in their actuality" (2001: 39). Further, in the "pulverized" space of postmodernity, space has become "re-territorialized in a way that does not conform to the experience of space that characterized the era of high modernity" (Gupta and Ferguson, 2001: 37). The re-territorialisation of space enables us to re-conceptualize the politics of community, solidarity, identity and cultural difference (ibid). While global cities may be prone to volatility, at the same time they also appear to generate often surprising new solidarities, new collective visions and new ideas about friendship and conviviality (Van der Veer, 2009). Diverse urban localities such as Bellville's central business district are representative spaces where struggles to achieve utopias may become realized (Parthasarathy, 2009).

5

The Boundaries of Citizenship

This chapter interrogates how contemporary notions of citizenship in South Africa influence the meaning of place in Bellville. As a place characterized by accommodation and safety for migrants – as opposed to exclusion and social disintegration for migrants – Bellville represents a place for the interrogation of citizenship. Conceptualized as a game of ever diminishing circles of inclusion, belonging may be performed in a space of a myriad of interconnecting local and global encounters such as Bellville. This chapter further situates Bellville, as a place of mobilities, in the context of generalized trends towards xenophobic violence in South Africa. It explores how conviviality emerges there out of shared understandings of citizenship and belonging. Notions of citizenship and belonging are central to the modus operandi, psyche and survival of migrants and elicit meaning about the role of place in Bellville. I question how notions of citizenship in Bellville are influenced by a habitus of mobility of its residents and of those they encounter. To what extent does habitus contribute to the emergence of conviviality?

5. 1 Opening Markets and Closing Doors

Notions of citizenship and of belonging to the nation-state are particularly significant factors influencing the degree to which conviviality emerges in Bellville. This is particularly so because of a history and manifestation of xenophobic violence in post-Apartheid South Africa. Political commitments of the South African state to determine who really belongs and who does not conjures a sentiment of suspicion that is often manifested through xenophobic attitudes and assaults aimed towards migrants. Opportunist attitudes towards non-nationals reflect societal perceptions of entitlement for citizens over non-citizens, and become "rationalized" because they are often committed by those in power. It was noted by Abdikadir that, "There is a lot of xenophobia, but it is especially directed towards Somalis because we are developing this country. We are changing things, creating our own futures. In this situation, there will always be opposition." Xenophobic tendencies feed into the "consciousness of the city" (Lefebvre, 1996: 80) and are clearly an outcome of a narrowly defined nation-state based citizenship (Nyamnjoh, 2006: 40). With trends towards xenophobia and other perilous outcomes emerging, it becomes necessary to reconsider the very notion of citizenship based upon the foundation of the nation-state, for its suitability to a world of mobility is fast becoming futile.

Many migrants moved to Bellville in search of security in the aftermath of xenophobic attacks. As Mohamed, head of the Somali Association of South Africa noted, "Many of us first moved to Bellville in 2006. In fact, this was when the xenophobic violence started, in Masiphumelele near Fish Hoek. We were targets so we had to leave." A report produced by the South African Human Rights Commission investigated the reasons for the eruption of public violence against non-nationals in South Africa two years later. In 2008, citizens murdered more than 60 people, raped dozens, wounded close to 700 and displaced more than 100,000, leading to a crisis of xenophobia in South Africa (Landau, 2011: 1). The report predicts that such targeted violence erupted due to several factors including: impunity and failure to maintain rule of law; competition for livelihoods and community resources; stereotypes about foreigners, including a lack of knowledge about the rights of non-nationals; and weakness in South Africa's immigration regime. Critically, the nature and reactions of grassroots leadership structures – their reactions to diversity coupled with imploding frustrations about inadequate service delivery and poor living conditions in informal settlements – may have been a tipping point leading to defects in the rule of law (SAHRC, 2010: 22). The politics of exclusion at many levels of government and society coupled with increasingly challenged notions of citizenship, belonging and access to state resources has led to systemic discrimination against non-nationals and "outsiders", particularly in communities of diversity. This has challenged the foundation of democracy in South Africa.

A failure to maintain economic conviviality has fuelled hostility toward migrants, as local shopkeepers – supported by local leaders – have retaliated due increased competition in the market, which is perceived as intrusion. Bloggers reacted in response to a television program about non-national shopkeepers,[3] noting that: *"The ppl grab everything 4rm us like job n business thy mus go back home n create their job opportunity we unemployed becos of thm!"* Another noted that, *"To tell de truth we as citizen, we are given a raw deal cause once u try and start ur small business there will be bylaws dat try and limit u but wen foreigners open business nothing is done to limit them. We are only told dat they are wat-wat seekers."* A further complaint was that, *"Spazas don't even pay tax, so what do they bring for us?"* A Somali man in Bellville analysed the situation as such,

"Why do people hold it in their hearts that they are still at war? There is a deep hatred, perhaps resting on the unsettled past and working into the unforeseen future. Is there hope in the future? Or is violence a response to a broken allegiance with hope, a raw and unforgiving truth that there is and will be competition for money, for shops, for the country. It is an attitude of *look at what my country has done for you.... And what about me?"*

Increasing social polarization has led to the formation of relatively autonomous sub and peri-urban communities across Cape Town. New urban spatial arrangements grow out of interpersonal networks and "embryotic" forms of self-organization have emerged as a symbolic form of resistance to a political economy that often excludes both foreign and local migrants (Campbell, 2006: 133). However, "cultural identities and assertion of difference do not

[3]"Trouble in Spaza" was aired by the local South African Broadcasting Corporation (SABC) on SABC 1 at 9: 30 p.m. on October 18, 2012.

necessarily result in urban conflict" (Myers and Murray, 2006: 11). In fact, conviviality often emerges from the search for autonomy, as demonstrated in Bellville. This upsurge emerges through varying trajectories in everyday life. In the context of Bellville, migrant-owned businesses provide work and income generating opportunities for South African job seekers, as well as low prices for local consumers, creating convivial relations. As a South African client reaffirmed, "These people give very good service, they are not ruled by their pride. You knock at their door at any time and are sure to get help. Most other shops you feel unwelcomed even with your money. " The dynamics of economic conviviality in Bellville run across the grain from national trends towards exclusion, as demonstrated by the alienation and aggression towards migrant shop owners in surrounding townships. Bellville is a place where conviviality emerges contrary to current citizenship trends, because people's relationships to citizenship have been tried and tested through migration and negotiations with the self on identity. "Where do I belong?" "What is my commitment to my country when it no longer serves me?" Where do my allegiances lie when home is no longer my place of birth or where I grew up, but where my family is?" Such questions of identity that emerge in the context of transnational migration have perhaps led many in Bellville to agree that, "Home is where I feel safe." I argue that this notion of safety – as an indicator of why Bellville has become home for a diversity of residents - leads to new approaches in conceptualizing belonging.

The sentiment of belonging in Bellville rests on a foundation of collectivity within individuality. Collectivity may be motivated by personal insecurity and communal desires for safety, perhaps generated by the uncertainties associated with mobility. The primordial desire for safety manifests itself because of the very nature of mobility that migrants in South Africa face. In a place where national reserve patrol commuter trains (Tyger Burger, 2012) and migrants claim, "you must ride in first class, or they may beat you up and throw you out the window", it is clear that daily mobility poses the potential for violence and intimidation. Drawing on Bourdieu's claim that, "The singular habitus of members…are united in a relationship of homology, that is, of diversity within homogeneity reflecting the diversity within homogeneity characteristic of their social conditions of production" (Bourdieu. 1990: 60) – a case may be made for a "collective" habitus. Safety emerges out of the diverse similarities (the homology) of people's negotiations with public insecurities. The emergence of safety in Bellville reflects the agency of individuals in reacting to collective concerns. Widespread concerns about safety generate a habitus of accommodation and hospitality that is manifested by the embodiment of collective social norms, understandings and patterns of urban public behaviour. This, perhaps, sheds light as to why migrants overwhelmingly describe Bellville as "safe". The notion of "collective" habitus in Bellville would likely be informed by common understandings of uprooted, transitory life and the insecurities endured. Safety in Bellville is, therefore, fostered by the experience of up-rootedness. It is fostered by the experience of having roots while uprooted, of creating new roots that extend the social boundaries of habitus to create not only a new self-position in "the game", but a new field for safer encounters that is Bellville (Bourdieu, 1994). Safety emerges when the collective interest in maintaining security outweighs underlying tendencies towards insecurity.

5. 2 Liminal Urbanity and the Challenges of "Belonging"

The rapidly increasing mobility of people nationally and transnationally has generated a powerful renaissance of the rhetoric of "belonging." Rooted in local politics, claims to belonging – and therefore to special rights to resources and freedoms – are not new, but have emerged with force in the latter part of the twentieth century. The importance of a localized (rooted) identity in the cosmopolitan age of urban migration creates a liminal space of the city, and Bellville is a place that is forever seen as one of temporary roots. Clifford's (1997) suggestion of "dwelling-in-travel" or "travelling-in-dwelling" describes the liminal zone of Bellvillê. For many, Bellville is a home away from home. It is a place that is characterized by temporary heritage, a chapter of one's life that concludes far from the city – either in a place called home or, for many, reunited with family regardless of locality. Many South African migrants in Bellville aspire to return to home villages such as in the Eastern Cape. Many Somalis in Bellville speak of their dreams of reuniting with family in the most unlikely of places – such as in the northern wintery state of Minnesota in the United States (Huisman et al, 2011). However, the importance of the village, the town or the city from which one's family hails remains critical to enhancing networks and associations, as well as identity politics in Bellville. While being "uprooted" – or mobile – propagates a greater inclusivity of belonging in Bellville, the importance of maintaining "roots" simultaneously creates circles of inclusion and exclusion.

This trend plays a critical role in Bellville, for the politics of belonging often negatively perpetuate the differences that arise from diversity, rather than celebrating the commonalities that arise through shared experiences in negotiating cosmopolitan space. The politics of belonging thus becomes embroiled in tensions that are often steeped in a politically charged history of shared memories of "us" and "them". Ethiopians and Somalis in Bellville, for example, continue to speak of their differences due to the 1977 war between those two countries – leading a majority of Ethiopians to settle in Johannesburg and a majority of Somalis in Cape Town. Exclusive claims of indigeneity, belonging and citizenship are often dependent on "historical amnesia" (Nyamnjoh, 2006: 80), and continue to represent challenges of belonging. Mobilities, and the emerging discourses of belonging that emerge concomitantly, lead us to consider how distinctions between home and travel may be reconceived. Mobilities in Bellville suggest that "home" is no longer the ground from which traveling departs and to which it returns. The idea of "home" may be broader than locality, extending to encompass ancestry, networks and the mobilities of modern families.

5. 3 Autochthony as "Authentic" Belonging

Despite increasing mobility within South Africa, a return to the local has led to increasing claims of autochthony, as societies seek to establish an irrefutable, primordial right to belong (Geschiere, 2009). Autochthony refers to the idea of "being born from the soil" – it is a deeply rooted concept representing the idea of "authentic" belonging. It is relational, reflecting bold statements of power that engender inequalities and politically charged attempts to exclude "outsiders". Autochthony manifests itself through socially tenuous and isolated positioning of migrants in South African cities. While Somali traders in Cape Town contribute to local economies – not only financially, but also by providing employment and entrepreneurial skills development to local populations - they face daily insecurity as their informal trading businesses (*spaza* shops) are targeted by competing South African traders. Criminal attacks on Somali shopkeepers are rampant, as they face the threat of opportunistic robberies, looting, orchestrated arson attacks and murders (Amit and Gastrow, 2012). Attacks are generally perceived by shopkeepers as imminent, and as a result, daily life is characterized by intimidation and fear. As Abdikadir, a liaison from the Somali Association of South Africa, noted, "This is not just robbery, this is hatred. Robbery is a matter of material possession, of ambush and theft. To shoot someone once you have all that you need from them, everything from their pockets but their life – this is hatred."Attacks against Somali shopkeepers that have left many killed, wounded or permanently disabled are but one example of violent exclusion.

Violence against foreigners is but one arm of the drive for autochthony, and demonstrates the "constant search for the exclusion of *strangers*" (Geschiere, 2009: 25) that takes place as a trend throughout South African cities. However, perceived "strangers" in South African cities are not exclusively migrants from other countries. Claims for belonging are often made within the framework of the nation, and are based on religion, ethnicity, clan, or language. Jonathan Klaaren notes that in the xenophobic violence of May 2008, one third of the victims were South African nationals, attacked because of their residential status (Klaaren, 2011: 140). Migrants in Bellville who travel to urban spaces for permanent, seasonal or informal employment and livelihood opportunities are also often the target of the politics of belonging. Urban space, a melting pot of people from different backgrounds, is often not considered to be "home" for foreign *or* local migrants, such as Sipho from the Eastern Cape who was searching for work in Bellville, or Patrick from Gauteng who works as a car patroller there. Migrants from within borders often maintain connections with home towns or villages in order to maintain an identity that is rooted to kinship history. This notion of identity is also deeply rooted in locality and place. It is related to the "necessity" of having a place of "origin".

Though not always associated with autochthony, regionalized hierarchies emerge in Bellville through identity politics related to ethnicity, religion and political power. This presented itself in Bellville when speaking to Patrick, a car patrol guard working on Durban Road who is originally from Gauteng. His anxiety of the taxi rank in Bellville described in Section 4.6, and his descriptions of the animosity and crime that he faces are evidence of such identity politics at play. Autochthony emerges in such instances based upon long-standing tensions related to imagined hierarchies amongst communities of different "roots". This leads us to question why and when identities in Bellville become, to use Arjun Appadurai's (2006) term, "predatory". Under what circumstances do certain notions of identity begin to refuse pluralist co-habitus with other identities? While I have attempted to address this question in terms of the dynamics of space, place and territorialisation in Bellville, it will need to be further addressed based on a critical overarching question for consideration: What are the conditions that make certain locations prone to violent intolerances (Landau, 2011a: 103), despite pockets of conviviality?

Autochthony has powerful emotional appeal as it is intimately linked to perceptions of individual and group identity. It renders identity fixed when it is actually always emerging. Bellville, on the other hand, demonstrates a metaphor for the fluid and interconnectedness of identity that emerges there to foster conviviality through habitus of accommodation (as opposed to resistance). This can be analysed through the different forms of music that are played in public areas throughout Bellville. Different business ventures boast a melange of musical tastes, as loud speakers individual to each shop project their daily rhythms. Music is played within the shops and is almost always audible from outside when passing by. While strolling down the street, one hears music from each shop in passing which fuse together – sometimes creating a musical conviviality and other times, cacophony. One may hear Somali music, South African national radio, electronic club music, women singing on the streets about a store's sale, and a diversity of sounds from circus music to Celine Dion's serenading prayers that project from a loudspeaker outside a local chicken eatery, Rasco's. In passing by, one takes what they please from each of these places, perhaps lingering at one to shop around if the music is particularly pleasing to the ear. Music in Bellville provides a metaphor for the idea that identity is circumstantial, spontaneous, even surprising at times. Conviviality emerges from such fluid approaches to identity. When the metaphor is posed towards approaches to national identity – which is increasingly based upon fitting into a mould of "insiderness" – one can imagine the hegemony of music that would fill our ears. A pity when there are many songs eager to be heard.

Figure 15: Loudspeakers Projecting Daily Rhythms

Vignette 5

Music in Bellville provides a metaphor for the idea that identity is circumstantial, spontaneous, even surprising at times. Conviviality emerges from such fluid approaches to identity

At Fashion City, a clothing store, there is a group of women standing around the sales baskets singing and chanting, rejoicing and celebrating loudly about a sale. Different women perform this in groups there daily. From one side I hear a South African radio comedy show being played. Another area has techno music, another plays Somali tunes. There is a giant loudspeaker outside of Rasco's Eatery. It is a prominent landmark, bright red in color, and was recommended to me as "the best place to eat." There is a man balancing his arm on the enormous speaker, claiming authority to the music that emanates throughout the entire area. He has a microphone in his hands and calls out to people passing by. "Where are you going, what do you need?" He asks me enthusiastically. The music man begins serenading the crowd with a blasting duet sung by Celine Dion and Andrea Bocelli, the English and Italian lyrics of this song, The Prayer, are ironically suitable to Bellville. *"Lead us to a place. Guide us with your grace. To a place where we'll be safe."* Such a diversity of music is spontaneous, out of place and surprising at times. Nevertheless, it is also tolerated by those who may not desire to hear it. The diversity of music is not resisted by complaints or allegations. In Bellville music is simply a true expression of individuality. It is a reflection of fluid identities in a global world. Conviviality emerges from fluid identities – learned in the face of up-rootedness.

Figure 16: Rasco's Restaurant and Music Ensemble

5. 4 The "Imagined Entity"

The nation state may be seen as an "imagined entity" (Harvey, 1996: 53) whose fate is, and has always been, in the hands of immigrants and diaspora communities. With this in mind, it may be said that the future of democracy in South Africa is particularly dependent on migrants' negotiations with the state, often facilitated by NGOs and local activists. The closure of critically located Home Affairs refugee reception centres in Cape Town – where refugees go to apply and renew immigration permits - is an example of South Africa's legal and administrative non-compliance to support refugees - an anomaly in its democratic discourse. This was discussed in Section 3. The closure of the centres is a bold signal to the international community about the role of the state in South Africa. Local NGOs have taken legal action against the state in the closure of the reception centre. Their activism on behalf of migrants in South Africa is paramount to civil society's negotiation with the state - and particularly in places such as Bellville where local governance and self-integration have proved the resilience and determination of migrants to succeed despite hardship. Relative autonomy in Bellville represents the possibility of promoting a more cosmopolitan democracy, one in which the current manifestation of ideas surrounding "the nation" themselves become history.

International migrants in Bellville lead us to consider the notion of "postmodern geographies", which require "a daily reinvention of new pathways for living" (Nyamnjoh, 2006: 81), such as through transnationally connected systems - *Hawala,* for instance - and clan based support amongst Somalis in Bellville. In doing so, new cartographies are imagined that inspire modern notions of citizenship and design our collective urban futures. Addressing increasing barriers to migration in an ever-more mobile world rests on a conceptualization of the idea of "flexible citizenship" (Nyamnjoh, 2006: 81). Flexible citizenship would be, as Francis Nyamnjoh writes, "Unbounded by the mirage of the 'nation-state' and its expectations of an impossible congruence between culture, race and polity"(ibid).

The emergence of mobility in Bellville provides a framework for imagining an embodiment of citizenship that is informed less by rigid geographies than by histories of relationships, interconnectedness, networks and conviviality. Flexible citizenship may take into account that migrants such as Aayan belong to numerous places. In a world of increasing mobility, nationality is truly a network of allegiances. For Aayan, these networks expand from Ethiopia, the homeland of her father; to Somali, the homeland of her mother and husband; to Kenya, where she grew up and left from recently; to various localities in America and Europe, where her extended family now live; and to South Africa, where she now lives with her husband and hopes to raise children. Alternative responses to the notion of citizenship are critical, as the world has become characterized by many "citizens" who exercise notions of citizenship in several countries. Imagining a more flexible citizenship regime allows us to make room for the possibilities of multiculturalism and cosmopolitan citizenship, characterized by global identities, in localities such as Bellville.

5. 5 Addressing the Urban Problematic of Belonging

Citizenship's commitment to the nation state has led to an "urban problematic" (Lefebvre, 1996) of belonging. This has perpetuated a discourse of "insiders" and "outsiders." Oftentimes isolated from the rights and privileges of society, "outsiders" have mediated social barriers in fluid and dynamic ways to produce identities that run across culture, language, city and national context. William, for example, is from Zimbabwe, though his military duties led him to Angola, Rwanda and the DRC as a peacekeeper with the African Union, a mission described as "like putting petrol on fire." He left the military and started teaching high school math in Zimbabwe. A lack of opportunity, let alone an invisible salary for his work – prompted his move to South Africa. At the time of our meeting, he was volunteering as an English teacher at the recently opened Bellville Education Centre, a school sponsored by the Somali Association of South Africa for the promotion of English language learning in Bellville. His broad travel experience, passion for teaching and many languages spoken sparked his interest in teaching Somali migrants in Bellville. Given a lack of commitment to locality and nation, individuals such as William may grow towards a transnational identity, in which notions of citizenship are not confined to nation state borders and civic duties are maintained along networks – such as networks of adult education that lead to Bellville - which transect localities. Appadurai argues that while individuals often identify with transnational cartographies, appeals of citizenship do necessarily attach them to territorial states (Appadurai, 2003: 346). This is reflective of the suggestion that:

"The ever surging communities of immigrants and diasporas globally mean that the 'nation-state' would have to reckon with a growing number of people who want not only the security and opportunities available in their countries of settlement, but also a continuing relationship with their country of origin and co-ethnic members (cultural kin) in other countries" (Nyamnjoh, 2006: 81).

The contemporary era of mobility has profound implications for growing networks of relations that are maintained across sovereign borders. While the discourse of globalization has long since initiated dialogue about global interconnectivity and interdependency from an economic sense, this discourse is yet to flourish in the contexts of citizenship and belonging. Trends towards migration are shifting modern notions of citizenship, leading to a test of the "salience of identity" (Delanty: 2000: 35) of the South African state, of Bellville's residents and of individuals linked to both.

5. 6 The Convergence of Conviviality and Cosmopolitanism

An analytical focus on conviviality in the everyday narrative of "insiders" and "outsiders" reflects upon the "salience of identity". It provides a contextual example of how society may organically conceive or inhibit cosmopolitan ideals of, in Immanuel Kant's term, the "right to hospitality" (Delanty, 2000: 56). Such cosmopolitan ideals are represented by post-national forms of inclusion and the enhanced interconnectivity of cultures (Delanty, 2000: 53), both of which are supported by community governance initiatives such as the Bellville Education Centre. The concept of cosmopolitanism is premised upon the assumption of what Lefebvre terms the "homo urbanicus", implying that, "City dwellers are atomised individuals with segmented personalities; that urban life recognizes the universal human by erasing differences; and that the city offers inclusive citizenship and the right to urban life" (Lefebvre, 1996: 97, 158; Jayaram, 2009). The point to be emphasized here is that community and cosmopolitanism are "polar tendencies" of the city, with the former implying an articulation of identity and collectivity and the latter implying an articulation of *multiple* identities and universal individualism (Jayaram, 2009). However, the due task of cosmopolitanism is to reconcile globalization and community (Delanty, 2000: 140). In order to mediate the two, it is necessary to emphasize that communities may become constituted and are not necessarily natural formations. The Bellville Education Centre, for instance, provides a site for inclusivity that is driven by convivial gestures of Somalis in Bellville through the Somali Association of South Africa. Conviviality is a critical notion in the development of community in Bellville, as it emerges through moments of (often spontaneous) inclusivity that may mature to represent cosmopolitan ideals (Frank and Stevens, 2007).

Conviviality in Bellville and its emergence in local forms further demonstrate the malleability of the boundaries of citizenship as well as the potential for "flexible citizenship" – a reading of citizenship whose relationship with the nation state is open-ended, cosmopolitan, and truly modern. By way of example, post-national citizenship commitments may be based on transcontinental "alliances and compromises" (Lefebvre, 1996). They may be based on T. H Marshall's idea that, citizenship is less a set of civic ties between the state and individual than a "bundle of rights" (Delanty: 2000: 14) that link the individual to the state. A vibrant civil society – formed out of a deep fusion of the political and the ethical (Arendt, 1958: 23) and of new possibilities for participation and rights beyond the state – may be the first steps to initiating a more "stateless society" (Delanty, 2000: 60). As Delanty argues, a transformation in democracy will need to take place for cosmopolitan political and social transformation to take root. While democracy *was* based on social integration; the roles of civil society, self-determination and the rule of law are *now* critical to encouraging multicultural pluralism and post-national identities.

5. 7 Capturing New Cartographies

Analysis of the outbreak of xenophobic violence leads us to consider that the marriage between citizenship and nationality is breaking down. As Gerard Delanty suggests, there is no longer a perfect balance between nationality – inferring membership of a political state community – and citizenship – as membership of a political civil society community (Delanty 2000: 19). It is in this context that it has become necessary to question new possibilities for citizenship, participation and rights both within and beyond state sovereignty, as well as the significance of increasing leadership and governance capacities of civil society in the absence of efficient and effective state government. Bellville provides examples of how citizenship may take new forms.

Given the tremendous degree to which borders and nations of the world today become unsettled, responses to global mobility and associated social changes must be cultivated through "flexibility". This concept expands on the notion that sincere conviviality in cosmopolitan space may emerge through de-territorialized modes of belonging. While citizenship is most commonly regarded as a territorially bounded concept, post-colonial citizenships are de-territorialized, maintained through travel, labour migration, forced upheaval, and multifarious residential patterns that traverse boundaries (McKinley, 2009: 56; Piot, 1999). A dilemma within the politics of belonging is taking place globally, fuelled by a redefinition of inclusion and civic duty in the context of a disintegrating relationship between nationality and territorially fixed identities.

Imbibed in chaos, this dilemma has, in many cases, led to a retreat back into the local that is represented by the drive to autochthony and is realized by the paradoxical outcome of human in-hospitability in a time of increasingly global economic conviviality. It is critical to conclude that, "A territorially bounded idea of citizenship in a world of flexible mobility can only result in policies and practices of confrontation that deny individuals and communities their realty as melting pots of multiple and dynamic identities" (Nyamnjoh, 2006: 75). Increasing flexibility on behalf of the nation-state through policies that encourage a network-based concept of citizenship may have the potential to capture new and emerging cartographies of geographies and citizens.

6

A Destination Reached?

There were, admittedly, countless directions that this study could have taken. As such, this book is reflective of my own personal perspective and experiences that emerged as I delved into this diverse and spatially-determined project. Many paths proved futile and others deviated from my expectations as I attempted to navigate my way through such a broad and encompassing study. In conceptualizing the research – of how conviviality emerges in the Bellville central business district, a global nexus for diverse populations and culture – I first had to define my own understanding of conviviality. A study of conviviality is not only relevant, but necessary, given the general focus of academia on the emergence of nativist sentiments – on violence and hostilities that emerge over social and political difference. A study of conviviality, on the other hand, requires a sense of optimism and subjectivity. However, there is a risk of being overly pollyannish in "finding" conviviality – avoiding the negative may imply that there is only positive, whereas conviviality is a fine balance between the negative *and* the positive. My assurance for "finding conviviality" was soon subdued, as I realized that studying conviviality also meant understanding why in some contexts conviviality doesn't manifest itself. In this study I have attempted to demonstrate that while Bellville does present opportunities for social cohesion and conviviality in diversity, it is also a liminal zone, created by people whose desire in the face of life threatening risks is to be "anywhere but here". Bellville is a transitory zone where hardships are often mitigated and safety is maintained. At the same time, it is a place where personal and collective social and political histories of migration are reminders of the violence and social exclusion that are daily realities for many migrants in Cape Town.

I threw myself into the void, initially allowing the realities of daily life to write the story that would become this book. Indeed, storytelling was an essential element in the collection of experiences, often through anecdotal experiences that helped reveal the social fabric and cultural background that produce conviviality. I observed my experience of space as I perceived it, and developed relationships as a participant observer, thriving off of daily life and its performances of personhood that we call culture. I realized the value of participant observation as a research method, for, as a stranger in Bellville, my senses became my method of assimilation. I observed my own negotiations with space through my role as a participant in it. I also relied on my own senses of space and place, and how they encouraged or discouraged the feeling of belonging in Bellville. As I socialized into the Bellville CBD – through convivial gestures of people such as Charles and Abdikadir who showed me around and made sure I always had a point of contact during visits – I experienced the spatial temporality of conviviality. I experienced and observed conviviality in the context of space and place and the meanings ascribed to defined territories within locality. Space and place, therefore, became core to my conceptual framework and understanding of conviviality, as is demonstrated in this book. Further, I have attempted to demonstrate how the intricacies of conviviality in Bellville may be represented through a tier of intertwined themes. These themes – including the micro-sociology of Bellville; the role of the state, of institutions and of the political economy; and Bellville from a global perspective – emerge throughout to portray a multi-level perspective of the dynamics of conviviality in Bellville.

This ethnography aims to portray not only elements of "thick description", but a conceptualization and a narration of the experience of migration (particularly for refugees) in South Africa. It demonstrates how encounters with the state confound the meaning of citizenship and how conviviality emerges from networks of social cooperation, despite grander narratives of social exclusion. As an ethnographic study of place, this book seeks to connect observations of space and place in Bellville to the context of a collective memory of violence against foreigners and South African migrants. The expansion and diversification of Bellville has generated new social relationships formed out of emerging mobilities. Negotiations over space, place, citizenship and belonging are reflective in physical space, and conviviality is shaped by unique spatial settings and urban forms in Bellville. Social space becomes embedded in physical place when efforts to achieve accommodation, tolerance and safety in Bellville are supported by social and physical negotiations over space. Public space plays a prominent role in mediating social and cultural differences. As such, the Bellville CBD demonstrates a unique and highly diverse urban context representative of patterns of conviviality. Bellville CBD is representative of the myriad of ways that urban public space may be instrumental in improving everyday lives. This is of particular significance to Cape Town, a city where a discourse of conflicting interests is frequently employed, and appropriation and use of public space is often contested by groups who want to assert their right to its use.

As a diverse urban public locality, Bellville exhibits a general sense of sociability, cooperation and entrepreneurial energy – such dynamics of the everyday encourage a greater degree of conviviality, though conviviality is not always emergent. In this book, I argue that conviviality emerges as a result of various interdependent ventures and negotiations of space and place that are often crafted out of mutual need. Chapter 4 – the ethnographic heart of the book -has sought to demonstrate how despite the continued narrative of "us and "them" in Bellville, conviviality emerges out of a negotiation of the destructive and a preference towards the constructive - out of the mutual benefits that arise from innovatively sidestepping away from tensions broiled in rhetoric of the "outsider". The potential for insecurity is either overcome or avoided by maintaining group identity and by engaging as intimate strangers, convivial to an extent that trust may reach. Conviviality emerges through collaborations between migrants and locals in economic ventures that lead to greater mutuality of interests; through transnational networks that are critically supported by ICTs; and through informal social rules that demonstrate places of interest and dis-interest in the context of mobilities within Bellville.

The Bellville central business district demonstrates the realities of interconnected local and global hierarchies of citizenship and belonging and how they emerge in a world of accelerated mobility. I argue that those who move - or are forced to move - may position themselves in relation to others with similar concerns, such as safety and protection. A common understanding of uprooted and transitory life, as expressed through habitus, therefore, unites a diversity of individuals around concerns for safety. Safety emerges when collective interests in maintaining security outweigh underlying tendencies towards insecurity. It is in this unique context that sentiments of belonging are negotiated amongst diverse citizens, whose accommodating of others is flexible to the extent that their own needs are secured too. Conviviality emerges through fluid identities that are formed by trends towards accommodation and hospitality; identities learned in the face of up-rootedness.

A study of conviviality and how it emerges in a diverse urban locality such as the Bellville CBD is of great theoretical relevance, as academics and policy makers attempt to understand global trends of urban migration and an ever increasing globalization of world trade. The dichotomy between the pace of economic and digital interconnectedness of global populations is contrasted with the slower pace of coming to terms with the physical movement of people in place and geographic space. There is a lag between realities on the ground and legal and theoretical frameworks for belonging. This study of Bellville hopefully sheds some light on how space and place impact urban socialization and conviviality in public places of mobility.

References

Abdi, Cawo Mohamed (2011). "Moving Beyond Xenophobia: Structural Violence, Conflict and Encounters with 'Other' Africans." In *Development Southern Africa* 29(5), 691-704.

Adey, Peter (2010). *Mobility*. London: Routledge.

Agamben, Giorgio (1995). "Homo Sacer: Sovereign Power and Bare Life." Giulio Einaudi. 1-98.

Ager, A. (1999). *Refugees: Perspectives on the Experience of Forced Migration.* New York: Continuum.

Akokpari, John K. (2000). "Globalisation and Migration in Africa." *African Sociological Review.* 4(2), 72.

Amit, Roni & Gastrow, Vanya (2012). "Elusive Justice: Somali Traders' Access to Formal and Informal Justice Mechanisms in the Western Cape." *The African Centre for Migration & Society* (ACMS). Research Report.

Amit, Roni (2011). "No Refuge: Flawed Status Determination and the Failures of South Africa's Refugee System to Provide Protection." *International Journal of Refugee Law.* 23(3).

Amit, Roni (2010). "Protection and Pragmatism: Addressing Administrative Failures in South Africa's Refugee Status Decisions."Johannesburg: Forced Migration Studies Programme, University of the Witwatersrand.

Amit, Vered (2002). *Realizing Community*. London: Routledge.

Anderson, Nels (1960). *The Urban Community: A World Perspective.* London: Routledge.

Ali, Ayaan Hirsi (2007). *Infidel.* New York: Free Press.

Appadurai, Arjun (2009). "Architecture and Amnesia in Modern India." Paper for the *Global Cities Conference.* Max Planck Institute for the Study of Religious and Ethnic Diversity.

Appadurai's (2006). "Grassroots Globalization and the Research Imagination." In *Anthropology in Theory.* Moore, Henrietta L and Sanders, Todd (Eds) 622-633.

Appadurai, Arjun (2003). "Sovereignty Without Territory: Notes for a Postnational Geography." in Low, Setha M & Lawrence-Zuniga, Denise (Eds). *The Anthropology of Space and Place: Locating Culture.* Massachusetts: Blackwell Publishing.

Appadurai, Arjun (1996). *Modernity at Large: Cultural Dimensions of Globalization.* Minneapolis: University of Minnesota Press.

Arendt, Hannah (1958). *The Human Condition.* Chicago: University of Chicago Press.

Barbour, B., & Gorlick, B. (2008). "Embracing the 'Responsibility to Protect': A Repertoire of Measures including Asylum for Potential Victims" (Report No. 159). Geneva: UNHCR, New Issues in Refugee Research.

Bauman, Gerd and Sunier, Thijl (1995). *Post-Migration Ethnicity: Cohesion, Commitments, Comparison.* Amsterdam: Het Spinhuis.

Block, Peter (2009). *Community: The Structure of Belonging.* San Francisco: Berrett-Koehler Publishers Inc.

Bohmer, Carol &Shuman, Amy (2008). "Politics Gets Personal." In *Rejecting Refugees: Political Asylum in the 21ˢᵗ Century.* New York: Routledge, 172-210.

Bourdieu, Pierre (1994). "Structures, Habitus, Power: Basis for a Theory of Symbolic Power." in Dirks, Nicholas B; Eley, Geoff; Ortner, Sherry B (eds). *A Reader in Contemporary Social Theory.* New Jersey: Princeton University Press. 155-199.

Bourdieu, Pierre (1990). "Structures, *Habitus*, Practices" *The Logic of Practice.* Oxford: Blackwell.

Buyer, Meritt (2009). "Negotiating Identity and Displacement among the Somali Refugees of Cape Town." In *South African Historical Journal* 60(2), 226-241.

Campbell, Elizabeth H (2006). "Economic Globalization from Below: Transnational Refugee Trade Networks in Nairobi. "in Murray, Martin J and Myers, Garth A (eds). *Cities in Contemporary Africa.* New York: Palgrave Macmillan.

Carvalhais, I. E. (2007). "The Cosmopolitan Language of the State: Post-national Citizenship and the Integration of Non-nationals." *European Journal of Social Theory,* 10(1), 99.

Castles, Stephen. (2002). "Migration and Community Formation Under Conditions of Globalization. " *International Migration Review.* 36(4), 1143.

Chambers, R. (1986). "Hidden losers? The Impact of Rural Refugees and Refugee Programs on Poorer Hosts. " *International Migration Review, 20*(2), 245.

Charman, Andrew & Piper, Laurence (2011). "Conflict and Cohesion in the Informal Economy: A Reassessment of the Mobilisation of Xenophobic Violence in the Case of Spaza Shops in Delft South Cape Town, South Africa." Working Paper.

Clifford, James (1997). *Routes.* Cambridge: Harvard University Press.

Clifford, James (1986). "Introduction: Partial Truths." In *Writing Culture: The Poetics and Politics of Ethnography.* Clifford, James and Marcus, George(Eds). Berkeley: University of California Press.

Cohen, Anthony (1982). "Belonging: The Experience of Culture" in *Belonging: Identity and Social Organisation in British Rural Cultures.* 1-17.

Copeland, Emily (2003). "A Rare Opening in the Wall: The Growing Recognition of Gender-Based Persecution." In *Problems of Protection: The UNHCR, Refugees and Human Rights.* New York: Routledge, 101-115.

Davies, Rebecca. (2007). "Reconceptualising the Migration-Development Nexus: Diasporas, Globalisation and the Politics of Exclusion." *Third World Quarterly.* 28(1), 59.

De Certeau, Michel (1988). *The Practice of Everyday Life.* Berkeley: University of California Press.

De Jong, Cornelius (1998). "The Legal Framework: The Convention Relation to the Status of Refugees and the Development of Law a Half Century Later." In *International Journal of Refugee Law.* 10: 4, 688-699.

De Fina, A., Nylund, A., & Schiffrin, D. (2010). *Telling Stories: Language, Narrative and Social Life.* Washington D. C: Georgetown University Press.

Delanty, Gerard (2000). *Citizenship in a Global Age: Society, Culture, Politics.* Buckingham: Open University Press.

De Vries, Marlene (1995). "The Changing Role of Gossip: Towards a New Identity?" in Bauman, Gerd and Sunier, Thijl (Eds). *Post-Migration Ethnicity: Cohesion, Commitments, Comparison*. Amsterdam: Het Spinhuis, 36-56.

Englund, Harri (2006). "Rights as Freedoms: Translating Human Rights. " In *Prisoners of Freedom*. Berkeley: University of California Press, 47-69.

Escobar, Arturo (2008). *Territories of Difference: Place, Movements, Life, Redes*. Durham: Duke University Press.

Esterhuizen, L. (2004). *Doing Case Studies for the Refugee Sector: A DIY Handbook for Agencies and Practitioners.* " The Information Centre about Asylum and Refugees in the UK, King's College: London.

Farah, Nuruddin (2000). *Yesterday, Tomorrow: Voices from the Somali Diaspora*. London: Cassell.

Ferguson, James (1999). *Expectations of Modernity: Myths and Meaning of Urban Life on the Zambian Copperbelt*. Berkeley: University of California Press.

Feyissa, Abebe & Horn, Rebecca (2008). "There Is More Than One Way of Dying: An Ethiopian Perspective on the Effects of Long-Term Stays In Refugee Camps. " In *Refugee Rights: Ethics, Advocacy, and Africa*. Washington: Georgetown University Press, 13-26.

Forsythe, David P (2001). "The Mandate of the UNHCR: The Politics of Being Non-Political." *Human Rights Working Papers*.

Foucault, Michel (2007). *Security, Territory, Population*. New York: Palgrave Macmillan.

Frank, Karen A & Stevens, Quentin (2007). *Loose Space: Possibilities and Diversity in Urban Life*. New York: Routledge.

Geertz, Clifford (2000). *Available Light: Anthropological Reflections on Philosophical Topics*. New Jersey: Princeton University Press.

Geertz, Clifford (1973). *The Interpretation of Cultures*. New York: Basic Books.

Geschiere, Peter (2009). *The Perils of Belonging: Autochthony, Citizenship and Exclusion in Africa and Europe*. Chicago: University of Chicago Press.

Geschiere, P. & Nyamnjoh, F. (2000). "Capitalism and Autochthony: The Seesaw of Mobility and Belonging." *Public Culture*. 12(2), 423.

Gilroy, Paul (2005). *Postcolonial Melancholia*. New York: Columbia University Press.

Green, Lesley (2008). "Crossing the Threshold of the Stranger: Ethnology as Professional Practice." Paper presented to the Potter Seminar on Fieldwork. University of Cape Town.

Gupta, A. & Ferguson, J. (2001). "Beyond 'Culture': Space, Identity and the Politics of Difference." *Culture, Power, Place: Explorations in Critical Anthropology* (3rd ed., pp. 33). Durham: Duke University Press.

Gupta A. & Ferguson J. (1997). *Culture, Power, Place: Explorations in Critical Anthropology*. Durham: Duke University Press.

Handmaker, J. , de la Hunt, Lee Anne, & Klaaren, J. (Eds.). (2007). *Advancing Refugee Protection in South Africa* (1st ed). New York: Berghahn Books.

Harvey, Penelope. (1996). Hybrids of Modernity: Anthropology, the Nation State and the Universal Exhibition. New York: Routledge:

Hillier, Jean & Rooksby, Emma (2005). *Habitus: A Sense of Place*. Burlington: Ashgate Publishing.

Hollenbach, David (2008). "Internally Displaced People, Sovereignty, and the Responsibility to Protect." *Refugee Rights: Ethics, Advocacy, and Africa*. Washington: Georgetown University Press, 177-193.

Huisman, Kimberly A; Hough, Mazie; Langellier, Kristin M; Tonor, Carol Nordstrom (2011). *Somalis in Maine: Crossing Cross Cultural Currents*. Berkeley: North Atlantic Books.

Human Rights Watch (HRW). June 2011. http: //www. hrw. org/news/2011/06/02/south-africa-open-new-johannesburg-refugee-center.

Illich, Ivan. (1973). *Tools for Conviviality*. New York: Harper & Row Publishers, Inc.

Jayaram, N (2009). "Revisiting the City: The Contemporary Relevance of Urban Sociology". Paper Presented at Conference: *Urban Aspirations in Global Cities,* Max Planck Institute for the

Study of Religious and Ethnic Diversity, Göttingen, 9-12 August 2009. Accessed online.

Jinnah, Zaheera (2012a). "Trading Places: Examining Somali Refugee Women's Lives and Livelihoods in Johannesburg." African Centre for Migration and Society Working Paper. Johannesburg: University of the Witwatersrand.

Jinnah, Zaheera (2012b). "New Households, new rules? Examining the Impact of Migration on Somali Family Life in Johannesburg." African Centre for Migration and Society Working Paper. Johannesburg: University of the Witwatersrand.

Jinnah, Zaheera (2012c). "Entering Sacred Spaces: Understanding the Meanings of, and Claims for Sexual and Reproductive Health Rights Amongst Somali Women in Johannesburg." African Centre for Migration and Society Working Paper. Johannesburg: University of the Witwatersrand.

Jinnah, Zaheera (2010). "Making Home in a Hostile Land: Understanding Somali Identity, Integration, Livelihood and Risks in Johannesburg." *Journal of Sociology and Anthropology* 1(1), 91-99.

Jordan, Bobby (2012). "SA Plans to Shut Refugees in Camps." Sunday Times. December 2, 2012. Accessed in hard copy.

Khan, F. (2007). "Patterns and Policies of Migration in South Africa: Changing patterns and the need for a comprehensive approach." UCT Refugee Rights Project. Working Paper.

Klaaren, Jonathan (2011). "Citizenship, Xenophobic Violence and Law's Dark Side." In *Exorcising the Demons Within: Xenophobia, Violence and Statecraft in Contemporary South Africa*. Ed Landau, Loren. Johannesburg: Wits University Press.

Landau, Loren B. (2011a). *Exorcising the Demons Within: Xenophobia, Violence and Statecraft in Contemporary South Africa*. Johannesburg: Wits University Press.

Landau, Loren B. (2011b). "Taming the Demons: Comparative Perspectives on Violence, Mobility and Diversity." SANPAD Concept Document.

Landau, Loren (2004). "The Laws of (In)hospitality: Black Africans in South Africa." African Centre for Migration and Society Working Paper. Johannesburg: University of the Witwatersrand.

Latour, Bruno (1999). "On Recalling ANT." In (eds) *Actor Network Theory and After.* Oxford: Blackwell.

Lefebvre, Henri (2004). *Rhythmanalysis: Space, Time and Everyday Life.* London: Continuum.

Lefebvre, Henri (1996). *Writings on Cities.* Ed. Kofman Eleanore and Lebas, Elizabeth. Oxford: Blackwell Publishers.

Lefebvre, Henri (1974). *The Production of Space.* Cambridge: Blackwell Publishers.

Loescher, Gil; Milner, James; Newman, Edward; Troeller, Gary G. (2008). *Protracted Refugee Situations: Political, Human Rights and Security Implications.* New York: United Nations University Press.

Loescher, Gill (2003). "UNHCR at Fifty: Refugee Protection and World Politics." In *Problems of Protection: The UNHCR, Refugees and Human Rights.* New York: Routledge, 3-18.

Loescher, G. & Mohanan L. (1989). *Refugees and International Relations.* New York: Oxford University Press.

Low, Setha M & Lawrence-Zuniga, Denise. (2003) *The Anthropology of Space and Place: Locating Culture.* Massachusetts: Blackwell Publishing.

Madhavan, Sangeetha & Landau, Loren B (2011). "Bridges to Nowhere: Hosts, Migrants and the Chimera of Social Capital in Three African Cities." In *Population and Development Review* 37(3), 473-497.

Malaquais, Dominique (2006). "Douala/Johannesburg/New York: Cityscapes Imagined." in Murray, and Myers (Eds). *Cities in Contemporary Africa.* New York: Palgrave Macmillan.

Malkki, L. H. (2001). "National Geographic: The Rooting of Peoples and the Territorialization of National Identity Among Scholars and Refugees." in A. Gupta, & J. Ferguson (Eds.), *Culture, Power, Place: Explorations in Critical Anthropology* Durham: Duke University Press.

117

Malkki, L. (1995). "From 'Refugee Studies' to the National Order of Things." *Annual Review of Anthropology, (24)*, 495.

Mackenzie, C., McDowell, C. & Pittaway, E. (2007). "Beyond 'do no harm': The Challenge of Constructing Ethical Relationships in Refugee Research". *Journal of Refugee Studies, 20*(2).

Mamdani Mahmood (1996). *Citizen and Subject: Contemporary Africa and the Legacy of Late Colonialism.* London: James Currey.

Marcus, George (1995). "Ethnography In/Of the World System: The Emergence of Multi-Sited Ethnography." *Annual Review.* 24: 95-117.

Mbembe, Achille (2000). "At the Edge of the World: Boundaries, Territoriality and Sovereignty in Africa." In *Public Culture.* 12(1): 259-284.

McKinley, Michelle A (2009). "Conviviality, Cosmopolitan Citizenship, and Hospitality." In *Unbound.* 5(55): 55-87.

Merry, S. E. (1984). "Rethinking gossip and scandal." In D. Black (Ed). *Toward A General Theory of Social Control. Volume 1: Fundamentals.* London: Academic Press, 271-302.

Miles, William F. S. & Rochefort, David A. (1991). "Nationalism Versus Ethnic Identity in Sub-Saharan Africa." *The American Political Science Review.* 85(2), 393.

Molotch, Harvey (1993), "The Space of Lefebvre." *Theory and Society.* 22(6): 887-895.

Monson, Tamlyn; Takabvirwa, Kathryn; Anderson, Jessica; Polzer Ngwato, Tara; Freemantle, Iriann (2012). "Promoting Social Cohesion and Countering Violence Against Foreigners and Other 'Outsiders': A Study of Social Cohesion Interventions in Fourteen South African Townships. African Centre for Migration and Society. Research Report.

Monson, Tamlyn. ,& Arian R. (2011). Media Memory: A Critical Reconstruction of the May 2008 Violence. In Loren B. Landau (Ed) *Exorcising the Demons within: Xenophobia, Violence and Statecraft in Contemporary South Africa,* Johannesburg: Wits Press.

Morgan, Marco & Guerrero Casas, Marcela. (2013). "Our Streets belong to everyone, not just those who drive cars" Marco

Morgan and Marcela Guerrero Casas. *Cape Times*. 21 January 2013. Accessed in hard copy.

Mpe, Phaswane (2001). *Welcome to Our Hillbrow*. Pietermaritzburg: University of Natal Press.

Murray, Martin J and Myers, Garth A (2006). *Cities in Contemporary Africa*. New York: Palgrave Macmillan.

Nicholson, Zara. (2011). "Bellville a Safe Haven for Somalis." *Cape Times*. May 11, 2011.

Niezen, R. (2010). *Public Justice and the Anthropology of Law*. Cambridge: Cambridge University Press.

Nyamnjoh, Francis (2013). "Fiction and Reality of Mobility in Africa" *Citizenship Studies*. 17(6-7):653-680.

Nyamnjoh, Francis and Brudvig, Ingrid (2013). "Conviviality and the Boundaries of Citizenship in Urban Africa" in *Handbook on Cities of the Global South*. New York: Routledge.

Nyamnjoh, Francis (2011). "Cameroonian Bushfalling: Negotiation of Identity and Belonging in Fiction and Ethnography." In *American Ethnologist 38(4), 701-713*.

Nyamnjoh, Francis. (2010) *Intimate Strangers*. Bamenda: Langaa Research and Publishing Common Initiative Group.

Nyamnjoh, Francis (2007a). "From Bounded to Flexible Citizenship: Lessons from Africa." In *Citizenship Studies*. 11(1): 73-82.

Nyamnjoh, Francis (2007b). "Towards a Predicament-Oriented Approach to Social Research Ethics." In A Rwomire & F Nyamnjoh (Eds). *Challenges and Responsibilities of Social Research in Africa: Ethical Issues*. Addis Ababa: Organisation for Social Science Research in Eastern and Southern Africa.

Nyamnjoh, Francis (2006). *Insiders and Outsiders: Citizenship and Xenophobia in Contemporary Southern Africa*. Dakar: CODESRIA Books.

Nyamnjoh, Francis. (2002). "A Child Is One Person's only In the Womb." *Postcolonial Subjectivities in Africa*. New York: Zed Books.

Nyamnjoh, Francis. "Production Legitimisation and Contestation of Culture: Of Games, Fields and Habitus, Pierre Bourdieu." Lecture Notes.

Nyamnjoh, Francis. "Clifford Geertz and the Birth of Interpretative Anthropology." Lecture Notes.

Nyang, SS (1994). "The cultural consequences of development in Africa." in Serageldin I and Taboroff J (eds). *Culture and Development in Africa*. Washington, DC: World Bank, 429–446.

Nyers, P. (2003). "Abject Cosmopolitanism: The Politics of Protection in the Anti-deportation Movement". *Third World Quarterly*, 24(6), 1069.

Omidian, P. A. (1994). "Life Out of Context: Recording Afghan Refugees' Stories." in L. A. Camino, & R. M. Krulfeld (Eds.), *Reconstructing Lives, Recapturing Meaning: Refugee Identity, Gender and Culture Change*. Washington D. C.: Gordon and Breach Publishers.

Overing, J. & Passes, A. (2000) *The Anthropology of Love and Anger: The Aesthetics of Conviviality in Native Amazonia*. New York: Routledge.

Parthasarathy, Devanathan (2009). "Rethinking Urban Informality: Global Flows and the Time-Spaces of Religion and Politics." Paper Presented at Conference: *Urban Aspirations in Global Cities*, Max Planck Institute for the Study of Religious and Ethnic Diversity, Göttingen, 9-12 August 2009. Accessed online.

Piot, Charles (1999). *Remotely Global*. Chicago: University of Chicago Press.

Putnam, Robert (1993). "The Prosperous Community: Social Capital and Public Life." In *American Prospect*. 4(13).

Ross, Fiona. (2010). *Raw Life, Good Hope: Decency, Housing and Everyday Life in a Post-Apartheid Community*. Cape Town: UCT Press.

Said, Edward (1979). *Orientalism*. New York: Vintage Books.

SANPAD. Conference on Migration, Conflict and Xenophobia. Rapporteurs' Summary of Key Themes. May 2011

Saniotis, A., & Sobhanian, F. (2008). "Polemics of Healing: Storytelling, Refugees and Futures." *Journal of Futures Studies*, 12(4), 1.

Scheurich, James. (1997). *A Post-modern Critique of Research Interviewing*. London: The Falmer Press.

Sharp, John, (2008). "Fortress SA": Xenophobic Violence in South Africa," *Anthropology Today*, 24(4): 1–3.

Sichone, Owen, (2008). "Xenophobia and Xenophilia in South Africa: African Migrants in Cape Town," In: Werbner, P. (ed.), *Anthropology and the New Cosmopolitanism: Rooted, Feminist and Vernacular Perspectives*, Oxford: Berg Publishers, pp. 309-332.

Smith, Merrill (2004). "Warehousing Refugees: A Denial of Rights, A Waste of Humanity." In *US Committee for Refugees: World Refugee Survey*, 38-56.

South African Human Rights Commission. (2010). "Report on the SAHRC Investigation into Issues of Rule of Law, Justice and Impunity Arising Out of the 2008 Public Violence Against Non-Nationals." Johannesburg, South Africa.

South African Government, Department of Home Affairs. (1998). *Refugee White Paper.*

Steenkamp, Christina (2009). "Xenophobia in South Africa: What Does It Say About Trust?" *The Round Table* 98(403), 439-447.

Steinbock, Daniel J (1999). "The Refugee Definition as Law: Issues of Interpretation." In *Refugee Rights and Realities*. Cambridge: Cambridge University Press, 13-36.

Steiner, N., Gibney, M. , & Loescher, G. (Eds.). (2003). *Problems of Protection: The UNHCR, Refugees and Human Rights* (1st ed.). New York: Routledge.

Sunier, Thijl (1995). "Disconnecting Religion and Ethnicity: Young Turkish Muslims in the Netherlands." In D. Black (Ed). *Toward A General Theory of Social Control. Volume 1: Fundamentals.* London: Academic Press, 271-302.

Sutton, Rebecca; Vigneswaran, Darshan; Wels, Harry (2011). "Waiting in Liminal Space: Migrants' Queuing for Home Affairs in South Africa." In *Anthropology Southern Africa* 34(1), 30-37.

Sztucki, Jerzy (1999). "Who Is a Refugee? The Convention Definition: Universal or Obsolete?" in *Refugee Rights and Realities*. Cambridge: Cambridge University Press, 55-69.

Somali Journalists Association of South Africa (SOJASA). "No Militancy at Our Mosques." Accessed via (http: //www. sojasa. com/?p=16.)

Tyger Burger. (2012). (Newspaper for Bellville and surrounds) "Metrorail increases security priorities. " July 23, 2012. http: //www. tygerburger. co. za/articles/articledetails. aspx?id=28468.

United Nations High Commissioner for Refugees (UNHCR) (2012). "Displacement: The New 21st Century Challenge." *Global Trends Report.* Accessed on 20July 2013. http: //unhcr. org/globaltrendsjune2013/UNHCR%20GLOBAL%20TRENDS %202012_V08_web. pdf .

United Nations High Commissioner for Refugees (UNHCR) (2006). *The State of the World's Refugees: Human Displacement in the New Millennium.* Oxford: Oxford University Press.

United Nations High Commissioner for Refugees (UNHCR). (1974). *OAU Convention Governing the Specific Aspects of Refugee Problems in Africa.*

Urry, John (2008). "Moving on the Mobility Turn." In (eds) Canzler, Weert; Kaufmann, Vincent; Kesselring, Sven. *Tracing Mobilities: Towards a Cosmopolitan Perspective.* Vermont: Ashgate.

Van der Veer, Peter (2009). *"Comparative study of Urban Aspirations in Global cities"* Keynote Address Presented at Conference: *Urban Aspirations in Global Cities,* Max Planck Institute for the Study of Religious and Ethnic Diversity, Göttingen, 9-12 August 2009. Accessed online.

Wright, Susan (1998). "The Politicization of Culture." In *Anthropology Today.* 14(1): 7-15.